THE MIDDLE ROAD

Amy Skinner

Cayuse Communications

www.cayusecommunications.com

The Middle Road
Written by Amy Skinner

First Printing -December 2021
Paperback ISBN: 978-1-7376150-3-3

0   1   2   3

Also by Amy Skinner

To Catch a Horse: Finding the Heart of Your Horsemanship

Find it at CayuseCommunications.com

Training horses is like climbing a mountain. There are different paths. If one doesn't work, go back and look for another way up.

—Kyra Kyrklund

Contents

About the Book

This book is not a training manual with step-by-step instructions. It is instead an honest, sometimes funny, and sometimes awkward window into the journey of a horsewoman. It prompts the reader to ask themselves questions, to evaluate and think a bit differently.

The book will take you through the messy parts of our personal lives with humor, insight, and a little discomfort. It offers support and connection to those who have felt alone in their struggles. It will help readers find strength from struggle, and sensitivity from the harsh and ugly realities we experience.

This book will also take you through the eyes of a horse—what they need, how they feel, and how we can best support them. By finding balance in our personal lives and within ourselves, we can cultivate something truly valuable to offer to a horse.

To Marlin

Many horses have come into my life to teach me. A few notable ones stand out that seemed to carry a united message: that I didn't know my backside from a hat and was clinging to a set of training ideals that didn't serve the horse. They wanted me to sharpen up, to pay attention, to listen to what they had to say. No horse in my life had said this with such clarity as Marlin. Marlin was strong, wild, and not to be intimidated. He was a horse that I have no doubt would have killed himself before submitting to any attempts to dominate him.

Marlin made it perfectly obvious when a person's nice speech and impatient methods weren't aligned. I watched in horror and amazement at how violently he would launch into resistance. He separated the true horsemen from the cowards, and the braggarts from the humble. Marlin bucked like no horse I've ever seen, he pulled back, reared, bolted, kicked, and made no hesitation to run someone down. His strength was formidable, his will was steely. There was no making Marlin do anything.

I was proud to own such a horse. I was amazed with his intelligence and self-preservation, and ashamed at what he'd revealed in me. Over the years, he became quiet, trusting, and soft, but mostly with myself and my husband. He was always wary of others and was quick to revert to self-defense tactics.

He'd sustained multiple injuries in his life—some from pathetic attempts at "making the wrong thing hard" in his training. Marlin made clear to these folks how puny their human strength was, and how willing he was to injure himself and others to get away. Facial nerve damage from a patience pole left his lip permanently droopy. Running through the round pen gave him scar tissue on his pastern. But, accumulated with the rest, the biggest injury that he sustained ultimately led to his passing. Out in the field he'd somehow ripped his side open from behind his shoulder to the point of his hip. We never found any evidence of where and how. Our vet stitched three layers deep with drainage tubes, and gave us a grim chance of his survival. If he did survive, she said, he wouldn't have much quality of life.

Months passed and he did heal, but over the years his balance was noticeably compromised. By the end of his life, he struggled to stand for trims or move comfortably. His hind end began to lose function, and he became increasingly nervous. Along with some pretty severe issues of hoof degeneration, Marlin was clearly no longer comfortable. We made the painful decision to let him go, over too long of a period of time.

On a rainy morning, I haltered him. He was quiet, easy to catch, and unusually cuddly. It wasn't like him at all to be affectionate, but this morning my tears flowed as he laid his muzzle over my shoulder, breathing softly into my ear. I wanted to interpret this as a sign he was comfortable with our decision, but I was overwhelmed instead with so much guilt. Why hadn't I taken better care of him? Why hadn't I handled him better? Why hadn't I learned quicker, instead of wasting so much of our precious short time together trying to "train" him? I should have listened more, relaxed more.

I remembered, that morning, the day of his first ride. His eye had become quiet, his lip soft. I brought my mare Dee into the round pen for support, and he rested his head on her back while I mounted. I rubbed his neck, and he stood quietly. The bucking, snorting, bolting horse was still in there, I knew that, and was smart enough at least to never forget it. But for now, he was trusting, and we shared twelve more beautiful and peaceful rides after that.

Along with our mare and his best friend, Dee, my husband and I led him out in the back field to graze where the grass was high and thick. Though he limped, he was so regal, stoic, and beautiful. The two horses touched noses, relaxed and grazed peacefully, and moments later he was laid to rest.

This book is dedicated to Marlin, who opened my mind to listening, who painfully exposed my ignorance, who forced me to think outside the box and experiment. Because of Marlin, I have been able to rehabilitate many more tricky horses who didn't fit into any category I would have previously known. Because of Marlin, I know that every horse can be peaceful when humans are peaceful, open, honest, and have the desire to get along with the horse above making horses obey.

A Dream of Horses

If you have horses in your blood, you know it's an incurable disease. The only relief for the ache is more horses. It's an affliction that can come on suddenly, with no warning. It may be genetic, but for some, its occurrence is just luck of the draw. And when you're the middle child of seven children in a horseless military family, the need for horses is like a thirst for water in a barren desert. Horses were my dream.

This dream carried me through my young life. Through the stress of frequent moving, constant change, new schools, new language, busy metropolitan cities, there was always the dream of horses. I couldn't quite make out what the cool kids were doing at the new school, my uniform wasn't right, and my teachers were frustrated with the curriculum I came with from my old school—but there were always horses.

In the bedroom of my tenth-floor apartment in Bogotá, Colombia, I could look out the window down to the street packed with cars, taxis, buses, and horse-drawn carts. Smog settled over it all in thick clouds. Dark clouds of exhaust billowed out of buses, but in between it all, the horse-drawn cart—the horse quietly providing transportation, income, and a spark of joy for that one person. A shred of hope and beauty in a sea of garbage, chaos, and noise. For a lover of animals and the natural world trapped in a high-rise cage, surrounded by sounds and smells that overwhelmed me, my small window of time with horses carried me through. It didn't matter if the horses were the sleek, well-fed Thoroughbreds I jumped at the military riding school or the bony nags tethered to the strip of grass on the highway. If there were horses nearby, I knew I could carry my dream alive.

As a young adult working as a stable hand, there was no peace and comfort like the sound and smell of dozens of hungry horses in a barn. The smell of dirty stalls or clean stalls, hay, shavings, the sound of running water, the little birds that made their nests in the barn, even the mice that found their daily feast in the feed room, all the sounds and smells of animals and nature were a joy to my senses. The barn became my church, and I became a devoted attendee to the temple where the sights, sounds, and smells soothed my jangled nerves and lifted my spirits.

Eventually I acquired my own barn. My daughter learned to walk in grassy fields. She wakes up every day to birds chirping, not buses and taxis honking. For her, a soft muzzle is always a touch away. It doesn't matter to me if she never rides or if horses don't stir her heart the way they have mine. But I'm proud to watch her grow with the freedom to be who she is, whatever that may be, surrounded by animals who offer unconditional caring. If she never chooses to ride, she will at least carry the strength and joy that horses so generously offer in the core of her being.

The Middle Road

One of the benefits I've had in my career is room to experiment. When I set out to become a trainer, with fresh ideas, a good back, and plenty of good, dumb hope, I had the sureness of a young idiot how horse training worked. I had studied with some world-renowned teachers, and some not as well-known but probably better horsemen, and I knew what was what. I had loads of experience with a wide variety of horses and a good understanding of a step-by-step plan.

The problem I very quickly encountered was that the horses I got to train didn't seem to adhere to my program. The folks who sent them to me rarely described them accurately. The six-year-old paint brought in for a tune-up turned out to be a killer who'd bucked off three other trainers. The friendly, seventeen-hand warmblood brought to get experience on the trail pulled back, broke halters, and kicked for shoeing. The steps I had in my mind didn't seem to be working the way I'd wanted them to. The horses I'd started under my teachers were unspoiled, relatively blank canvases, with good temperaments for the most part. The ones I was getting in training were outlaws described as cream puffs, horses that bucked, pulled back, bolted, and reared. They were destined to be grandma's horse with a 30-day training budget.

My eagerness to prove myself as a horse trainer was exceeded only by my need to pay bills. My overhead was climbing steadily, with the addition of a truck, trailer, and repairs for what the 30-day outlaws were wrecking. Barn doors were broken down, trailers dented, and fence boards busted. I was hungry to learn more, to do better, and I was actually just downright hungry. I was finding less success in the methods I'd studied than I expected, and personal and financial issues caused me to bounce from teacher to teacher for years.

In retrospect, never latching to a certain style of a particular teacher over those years was a blessing in disguise. I'm reminded of a drawing course I took during my brief stint in college. My teacher would lecture on how to draw the human form, still life, foreshortening, buildings, and then present us something entirely different to draw. Dumbfounded, I'd stare blankly at my easel after drawing a wimpy outline. Afraid to further ruin my drawing already destined for failure, I was paralyzed. "When you don't know what to do," my teacher had said, coming around to see our work, "do something. Anything."

I didn't know what to do with these horses. I got bucked off, kicked, bolted with, trampled into the dirt. I was in prime shape to experiment, and experimenting is what I started doing. I started letting go of my ideas of what horses "should" do and started realizing, through the help of some outlaw equines, that they in fact don't have to do anything I want them to do. My frame of mind started shifting away from getting horses to do things, and more toward seeing what would happen if I changed my expectations.

I realized I didn't know what I was doing and decided to shake it up and do some experimenting. The horse I'd been trying to teach to stand while mounting, I suddenly just let walk off. When I tried to stop him, he bolted anyway, so I just let him go. We galloped away from the mounting block a few times. The third day he broke into a trot and then down to a walk shortly after mounting. On the fifth day, he just stood there.

In some ways, my work became a mess. Horses were walking all over me. My students were frustrated and confused. While I didn't yet have a good handle on what I wanted to do or how, I knew I was onto something. Everything was in absolute turmoil, because I knew what not to do anymore, but didn't know what TO do. But one thing was going very well— horses were much less interested in trying to use their power and strength against me.

As time went on and I started bringing troubled horses along with more success, I started getting them for longer periods of time. The colts that I started and kept, months later, were showing me the obvious flaws in their beginning as I tried to advance them. I was starting to see the gaps that come from the result of immediate-fix-inspired training, and this was giving me a huge advantage toward my work with new horses.

I ran the gamut of extremes: too authoritarian, then too passive. In horse care as well, I was the same. Never stalls, never blankets; never grain, never shoes. Then I got horses who were sore, cold, and underweight. Next I coddled my horses and created in them the inability to adapt—they became spoiled and soft. Over the years I started looking a bit more at the big picture. I no longer threw the stall baby out to the field to fend for himself, but introduced him more slowly. If they shivered, a stall or a blanket was helpful until they warmed up. If they spent their life in shoes, they remained in shoes or at least with boots.

Of course, I didn't learn all the important things alone. They say when the student is ready, the teacher will appear. I found two excellent teachers after much personal pain and suffering with other teachers: Theresa Doherty, a longtime student of Walter Zettl and Egon von Neindorff, who possesses the sharp eye for equine and human balance, and Brent Graef, with an almost wizard-like ability to read and communicate quietly with horses. One dressage rider, one Texas cowboy. Each having totally unique experiences, lifestyles, and methods for handling and caring for horses, but both intensely dedicated to the well-being of the horse, they offered me a perspective I desperately needed—the middle road.

I think there is a very interesting line between a dictatorship with the horse and avoiding anything that makes them uncomfortable. Because humans are humans, we tend to go to extremes. There are some people who treat their horse like a tool. They're likely to say "He has to do x, y, z," and "I expect my horse to do x, y, z." Then there are people who say "My horse doesn't like that, so we don't do it . . . He is scared to be tied, so I don't do it . . . When I went out to catch him, he said 'no thanks,' so I didn't bother him."

As with anything, the healthy approach is the middle road. If we force our horses to do our bidding without regard for their feelings, there obviously is no room for a real relationship of any kind. To some people, the horse is a toy they purchased to do what they want. What a sad existence for a horse.

For the folks who never ask their horse to do anything uncomfortable, the horse never learns any structure and isn't able to gain confidence. They might say no initially because they worry, don't understand, or don't have the tools to complete the task. It's our responsibility to give those tools to build a horse who has confidence in themselves, in us, and in the world at large. A horse who doesn't expand their comfort zone is at high risk—how will they get shots, trims, tie if needed, or be handled by a vet, caught in an emergency, hauled to safety? How will you keep them sound over their riding life if they "don't like ring work" or don't want to change their posture? How will you keep them safe, sound, and happy if they can't try new things?

Building a horse who is habituated to say no is not ethical, just as creating a soldier for a horse is not ethical. It leaves them vulnerable, without tools to deal with their world, and unless you plan to set them free into the wild, they still have to deal with the elements of domesticity that aren't natural for them.

I try to give all my horses the tools they need to be confident, to be safe, to handle the unexpected, and I respect when they say "No, I don't want to do that." But hearing no means I need to evaluate: Do they have the tools they need? Do I need to approach this differently or at a different time? And, yes, sometimes what I'm asking isn't appropriate. If it doesn't improve the horse's life, I think they have a right to say no. But if I know it will add value to their life, I need to find a way to help them get confidence enough to do it.

As with all elements of a partnership, I listen to their concerns and introduce things in a way that suits them. The truth with horses, as with life, is rarely in the extremes, but more often found in the middle.

Opportunity Does Not Come Knocking

All I ever wanted to be was a horse trainer, since I was a little kid. As a seven-year-old, I wrote out my step-by-step plan for getting to my horse training Shangri-la, beginning as a stable hand, then making the step toward exercise rider, with a brief detour to become a ballerina, a farmer, and an astronaut, then on to be a jockey, and finally a horse trainer.

My focus has largely been laser sharp toward this goal throughout my life. As I got older, I willingly let go of my ballerina and astronaut dreams, grew out of the upper jockey weight limits by 13, and mourned the loss of the farming dream. But from a young age, I was working toward my goal: working off lessons by cleaning stalls, hanging over fences to watch lessons, and pestering trainers to ask The Big Questions.

It wasn't a straight shot or as easy as I thought. I moved around so much as a kid, and each new barn I found myself in had an entirely different discipline, culture, and philosophy. By the time I had adapted to one and figured it out, I was at a new one. Suddenly my outfit was all wrong and I needed new clothes; the way I led, saddled, bridled, and rode was all wrong. I constantly had to start over. One example of this was an entrance test at a lesson barn I had to take to place me in the correct riding level group. They asked me questions like "Do you know your posting diagonals? Do you know your leads?" I shook my head, having never heard these words before. I had learned to ride in Spanish, and diagonals and leads were unfamiliar words to me. Only after being placed in a beginner's class after many years of riding did the meaning of those words click for me. After spending months with a disinterested instructor droning "up-down, up-down" at a group of us in the arena, I was allowed to progress to the novice group. I started all over, moved up a level, then my family and I moved away again.

As an adult, sticking to my plan toward training horses was immediately more difficult. I didn't grow up in a horsey family and suddenly came to find out horses were very expensive. I had no car, no money, no horses, and no access to horses. I was barely keeping rice, beans, and ramen in stock, so riding my bike to the local barn for a weekly lesson was just not something I could see happening.

As luck would have it, while living in Tallahassee, Florida, I got hired to mow pastures a few days a week at a dressage barn just on the southern border of Georgia. I found this gig from an ad on Craigslist and made every effort to overrepresent my ability. George, the owner, was a retired jockey and looked every bit as worn out as I'm sure he felt. His skin had been punished by the long, sunny southern summers, and his body had no doubt been punished by many hot-tempered racing horses. George was grumpy, walked with a limp, and fought over hiring me with his wife within earshot of me, but he gave me a shot.

The look of disdain over his face when he sat me on his John Deere tractor still makes me chuckle to this day. I didn't know how to drive a tractor, I didn't know how to shift gears, and I had neglected to tell George I could barely drive. My then boyfriend had driven me to the farm and would pick me up, since, at 19, I didn't even have my driver's license yet (one of the side effects of going to high school overseas). George showed me how to drive the old tractor and unleashed me to wreak havoc on his fields.

Over the months that I was there mowing, I got more comfortable with the horses nearby, as I often had to move them from one field to another to mow. George's wife, Linda, generally avoided eye contact with me or gave me a passing sneer. But magically, over time, some of the boarders, for God knows what reason, began asking me to ride their horses. Maybe I was just in the right place at the right time, or maybe it was a testament to human stupidity, but people who didn't know anything about me or my ability (which was nil) gave me the keys to their tack lockers and the halters to their horses.

I exercised a nice Appaloosa named Sparky, a quarter horse named

Tex, and an Arabian cross named Windy. Heaven was riding these horses. I didn't know much other than how to mostly stay on, although by now I was sure what a posting diagonal was and what a lead was. Their owners never watched me ride, so I had lots of time to experiment, bounce around, make mistakes, and come onto some cool realizations, wandering alone with a horse in the hot Georgia sun. Eventually, my then boyfriend got sick of driving me to and from the Georgia border. I lost the job, dumped the boyfriend, got my driver's license and a used car, and moved back in with my parents in Virginia.

I got my first job cleaning stalls at a lesson barn in Virginia by again overstating my experience and ability. I was a beanpole unaccustomed to physical labor, but this job was my dream come true. Bucking hay bales, hauling water, cleaning stalls, and all the other ins and outs of daily horse care led to a type of soreness and exhaustion I had never experienced. The blisters, the sore muscles, eating two hamburgers and a carton of ice cream for dinner and still being hungry (those were the days).

The second day of work I was so sore I thought I would quit, the third day of work I was more sore than the second, but by the second week, I was feeling stronger than I'd ever been in my life. Looking over a clean barn, hearing 40 horses eat hay, and watching them drink from clean buckets and roll in good, clean dirt in a pasture I'd just picked gave me a type of pride and confidence I'd never felt before. I never felt a sense of belonging anywhere I'd lived, but I belonged in a barn. No matter where it was in the world, no matter what language was spoken or what halters were used, as long as horses needed feeding and care, I felt like there was a place for me.

I moved again, this time to Michigan, and found another place to clean stalls. But still I wanted to train horses. I rode lesson ponies with behavioral problems off the clock. I got bucked off, stomped on, run off with, bit, kicked, and more things horses invented on the spot. I scrounged up the money to do paid internships. I started taking lessons. I volunteered for equine rescues, training horses just for the practice. I worked for free. I scraped by. After a while, I wound up with a training position at my Michigan barn and spent most of my time working with problem horses and young horses. I learned a lot, made plenty of mistakes, and started to get the unfortunate and misleading sense that I knew what I was doing.

I rode with every clinician who came into town and drove miles to others. I kept working hard, riding horses no one in their right mind would touch in the timetable I was given. I got injured, healed, and worked some more. Eventually, I wanted to move beyond just problem horses and young horses. I'd had some dressage lessons before, probably just enough to become dangerous to every horse I met, and decided that was what I wanted to do. I applied and, miraculously, through overvaluing my experience level and ability, was accepted into La Real Escuela in Jerez de la Frontera, Spain.

I saved all my money, and the boarders at my barn all chipped in to buy me a pair of nice tall boots. A friend of mine gave me nicer breeches than the threads I was wearing, presumably so I wouldn't bring shame to America, and off I flew. I stayed in a five-star hotel there within walking distance of the school. I had used up all my money, and for the rest of the trip I ate one can of beans or a loaf of bread a day and washed my clothes in the bathtub, using the hotel dryer to dry them.

At school I would draw a crowd—the other students would gather to watch me get yelled at. As I walked down the hall toward the barn, I could see the boys looking at the posted schedule, searching for my rides for their entertainment. My instructors would yell and cuss. "Have you never ridden before?" "You ride like you're having a seizure!" There were a lot of swear words I had to look up after my lessons. I learned to ride through the pressure of snickering boys and eyes watching me, and how to hold in tears until I got to the bathroom.

In the end, I bought my own farm, essentially through overstating my financial stability and ability to be an adult. Having a mortgage to pay is an enormous motivation to get yourself out there, work hard, learn more, but also to charge what you're worth, to be confident enough to get what you need to feed your family. There is no wimping out with a hungry toddler and a farm to take care of—any lack of confidence to go out there and get what I deserve, what I need, affects my family and my ability to take care of them.

It's been extremely satisfying, but I wouldn't say it's been comfortable, by any stretch. I've slept in my car. I've gone without meals. I've left boyfriends and moved across the country for my career. I've lost friends. It never got easier, but I got more accustomed to discomfort.

Opportunity does not come knocking, waiting patiently for you to answer. The stars don't often align, and sometimes there is no magic place where you belong. You won't always be in the right place at the right time or be rewarded by the universe for your devotion. You might have to put on your Carhartt bibs and smash the door down with a sledgehammer. Then once you're in, you work every single day constructing a place that you can belong to.

The Ball Hitch of Life

I like to think I have a lot of patience and the ability to stay calm in the face of distress. One scenario it turns out I do not have this ability in is backing up the truck to the ball hitch of my bumper pull trailer.

I trailer out a lot, so you'd think I'd have this skill down pat. There are these two little marks I've made on the bed of my truck that are supposed to guide me to the ball hitch. If I line these little marks up just right, it puts the ball hitch right in the middle of them. I never trust these marks, though. If I have plenty of time, I do pretty well. If I'm in a rush, things can get messy. I put my truck in park, get out to evaluate where I am in relation to the ball hitch, and find I'm off the mark by an inch to the right or left. So I get back in the truck and make my adjustment, put it in park again, and find that I'm off an inch in the other direction now. I repeat this several more times until comes the pivotal point where I have to make a decision: Is this salvageable, or do I need to pull forward and start over?

I have a strong work ethic, I tell myself. My parents didn't raise a weakling! I can make this work. By the time the ball hitch is under the trailer hookup, it's off to one side. Still convinced I can make it work, I find myself trying to force the trailer hookup over the ball hitch with brute strength. I say every curse word I know and make up some more. Sometimes a good kick to the trailer tongue forces the trailer into submission, though a shin or foot bruise usually ends up being the high price I pay. And where is my husband?? He is probably playing *Candy Crush* on his phone in my time of distress.

I was having a conversation with a friend about her trailer, and we somehow ended up on the subject of my cursing, kicking, brute-force-using hookup methods. "Why don't you just pull forward, straighten out, and start over when you're a little better set up?" she said, laughing at my unique way of working. I thought about it and realized I didn't have a good answer. It would save more time to just start over, instead of hitting my head against the same wall repeatedly.

Then I thought back on several painfully similar instances in my life, where instead of "pulling forward and straightening out," I just kept throwing more work, more money, more effort at the same problem. "Oof," I said. "I think there's a pattern here," she said, laughing. Maybe the big changes in our lives are, in reality, made up of how we approach small mundane things. Maybe if I can straighten out my trailer hookup, I can straighten out my life. Who knows?

The High Road

Taking the high road with horses means listening to the horse above all: above show agendas, demos, makeovers, clinics, and time constraints. It means taking however long the horse needs, not the guidelines set by rule books or impatient riders.

The high road is unpopular. It might mean your demos are about as exciting as watching paint dry while you wait for a horse to relax. The high road might mean scratching on a dressage test because the horse is anxious, tired, or sore. It might mean losing work or turning a client away whose desires are unfair to the horse.

Putting horses first has no rules, no steps, no levels, except listening to the horse. It means going by feel and being open to changing our ideas. It means doing things we didn't expect to do, or maybe hadn't wanted to do. The high road might cost you everything. It doesn't necessarily bring in money, fame, recognition, ribbons, or medals.

It doesn't always even bring peace of mind. You might lie awake at night, troubled by the things people said about you, or the horses taken to other trainers who made promises of faster or flashier progress. You might worry about the well-being of horses frequently and overstretch yourself to care for them. You might lose clients, money, and sleep. You might sweat, cry, and struggle. The high road is exhausting and lonely.

The high road is open to everyone. What it has to offer is simple and real. For every ribbon forfeited and dollar lost, the joy of a soft muzzle and relaxed breath is priceless. Its real reward is peace with horses and skills that are yours alone—skills that no one can take from you. The horses you work with become your true friends and will give more back to you than you ever thought possible. They will offer everything they have and more, and at times it might not be what you wanted to get, but what you needed to get. The horses you know can be your guides in personal development, showing you how to be honest, trustworthy, and patient, and how to let go of what doesn't matter, what doesn't serve you, and what impedes your progress.

The world may not reward you, but each and every horse you encounter will give you more than money could ever buy, if you're open to the quiet gifts of the horse.

Toughen Up!

"If you want to be a horse trainer, you've got to toughen up!" I can remember hearing that over and over. My instructors would say that as they kneed my lesson horse in the gut while cinching up. "They're big and you're small! There's nothing you can do to hurt them." They would say that while putting on correction bits, tie-downs, bigger spurs. As if sensitivity was a burden, not an asset.

The whites of the eyes, flared nostrils, labored breathing of the hobbled, tied-down, panicked horse haunt me still. I can smell his sweat, hear the whip crack, and I can still hear the incongruent words smoothing it over, explaining it away. "He isn't scared, he's just being stubborn." Part of me prayed he would just lie down, get it over with. The other part of me prayed he'd jump out of the round pen and never be seen again.

"You've got to toughen up!" I was told when riding a bronc-y young horse who probably was nowhere near ready to ride. "You've got to toughen up!" I was told on my way to the hospital. "You've got to toughen up!" they said when I lost all confidence. "You've got to toughen up!" they said, and you shouldn't care when clients choose the wrong path for the horse you've worked with and come to love. It's a money game, so I shouldn't care, and you can't save them all, right?

The further I delve into this, the more I see the value of sensitivity. Being receptive to the smallest details of equine expression has launched me into a deeper connection with horses than I ever thought possible. Noticing the breathing, the way they blink, the sound of their footfalls, the movement of their tails, the way they hold their skin—these details are the key to a real conversation with the horse. A lack of sensitivity, a false sense of "toughness," deprives a person of the ability to really be in the moment with the horse. When you're so busy "training," so sure of what the horse is thinking or saying, without the sensitivity to actually listen, you can never get more than mechanical responses, submission from some—but there are the outliers: the horses who won't ever back down, won't ever quit. The person lacking sensitivity blames the horse and misses the chance to really talk to the horse, or to anyone, for that matter.

I am overly sensitive. I'm not that brave and not that tough. My sensitivity alerts me to when something is wrong with the horse. My cowardice prevents me from riding a scared horse and makes me more committed to having a good foundation, a good base of communication going, before I push my or my horse's boundaries beyond repair. My sensitivity helps me experiment, to listen to what the horse really needs.

You can teach people technique, you can teach them theory, but you can't make anyone have empathy. As a teacher, I find it pretty obvious who has it and who doesn't. My husband always says, "Would you want to be taught that same way?" A horse is not some machine devoid of feelings, though they aren't human and don't have human emotions.

Empathy is what separates the surface workers from the real deals. And to those teachers who warned me to toughen up, I say I have. It takes guts to go against the stream, and it takes guts to feel what your horse feels, especially when you've caused it.

Am I Safe?

One of the things I have focused on in my work with horses is helping them answer the question "Am I safe?" at the very beginning of each ride. My friend, neurologist Steve Peters, helped me understand this point, and since then, it's been a central focus of my warmup with each ride. But two clinics recently drove home this point for me as a teacher of humans. In order to optimize our learning, we need to feel safe too.

It was sunny and cold. My husband, students, and friends were lined up outside the arena to watch me ride with a well-known German instructor. The horse I was riding was stiff from being stalled for a few days. As I warmed him up, I felt the issues he'd been sent to me for training return: anxiety about cantering, specifically around flying changes, and stiffness in the neck and bridle. I hadn't asked for a flying change in the warmup, but asking him to canter brought out his anxiety in anticipation of doing a changeup. So, I spent some time trying to get him relaxed in the walk and trot before the lesson.

In my lesson, one exercise quickly went sideways—literally. It involved quick transitions from a trot leg-yield to a canter with a five-meter half-circle turn. My horse's anxiety escalated and he began cantering sideways. The instructor said, "More inside leg!" I became more tense and suddenly became very aware of the people watching the mess unfold. I worried about what they thought, what the instructor thought, and I worried I was ruining this nice horse. By the end of the lesson, I hadn't gotten the situation straightened out, and I felt totally defeated. My friends and students had watched me fail. I'd failed the horse. And I was questioning whether I should even teach anymore. My next lesson went a little better, but my heart had sunk and my desire to try was depleted.

The following week, I was scheduled to ride with Mark Rashid. The anxiety crept back up. What would my students think of my ability? What would the auditors think—my clients and local people—would they talk badly about me? I brought my own horse this time. Would his issues make me look bad? What would Mark think of me? I did my best to take some deep breaths and quiet my mind before riding, but the anxiety sat with me as I began my lesson.

My horse was stiff, anxious, and calling for my other horse I'd brought along. Mark watched me warm him up and asked me questions. My shoulders were tight. I tried to stay with my horse, forget about the students of mine watching, forget about the local trainer in the doorway, and just focus on my horse. I was sure Mark could see and feel the mess I had going on in my head, because he took some time to talk with me, throw in some compliments about my riding, and explain things in a positive way. His presence was peaceful and nonjudgmental. I didn't feel like he treated me any differently than anyone else. He was here to help whoever wanted to be helped.

I started to relax some, and I was able to ride my horse. He gave input and direction in a way that helped me make changes with my horse. My confidence started to come back. Within a few moments, I was back to myself again, just riding my horse with some good help. My gelding started breathing, letting go of the tightness in his back, and loosening up. The little things were working better, and I felt I had achieved something.

I drove home that night thinking about how much a teacher can affect the confidence of their students. For us teachers, it isn't enough to just know a lot. A good teacher teaches to the students' needs. They make it possible for students to succeed, even if only in baby steps. They break things down and find ways to explain the building blocks of any given exercise. When things don't work out, they break it down even more, or move on to something else.

The lessons I had were an incredible reminder in how important it is as a teacher to help students feel safe, physically and emotionally. To feel safe to try, comfortable enough to learn. Just as a horse isn't able to learn when anxious or uncomfortable, a student's mind is not open when they feel defensive, scared, or anxious. A good teacher can help bring peace to the rider, so that they in turn can offer it to the horse.

The late American spiritual teacher Ram Dass said, "When you know how to listen, everyone is the guru." The first lesson was a great experience in empathy for my students who experience this worry in lessons. The second was a wonderful lesson in how much learning can take place when the mind is quiet. So, as I go about my teaching now, I will work harder to protect and develop the confidence of my students and to help them answer the question "Am I safe?"

Helping Horses, Helping People

The big names in our horse world can hold a crowd. They talk up their program and like entertaining. Making connections, for them, seems to come naturally. But as an introvert, being a horse trainer can be difficult. The horses are not the problem. Interactions with people are.

I don't dislike people or dislike being around them. But I'm easily overstimulated by too much noise, especially talking, and I feel much more comfortable alone or with one or two people. I don't love to schmooze crowds, talk about myself, or entertain people. Training horses called to me because of the quiet, peaceful interactions I could have with horses. Going all day without talking to anyone while I worked and rode was and is my idea of heaven.

Now I know that being a professional is much more than isolated horse work. One is often approached by strangers. Client relationships are often about much more than their horses. People also need to just talk with someone, sometimes about things personal and unrelated to riding. Initially, I was puzzled by this phenomenon of sharing deeply intimate information. I might be working with someone's horse, explaining what my work was aimed at doing, and they might begin to talk about their childhood trauma, messy divorce, or other heavy emotional load. I encountered it frequently, and at the time, it seemed irrelevant and distracting to the task at hand.

I talked to a clinician friend of mine about it. He was older and more savvy, and he understood my preference for the peace of quiet horse work and the outdoors. In his mind, folks were coming to clinics not just for horsemanship but because they were dying for some type of connection. Being horseback made them feel vulnerable. The reasons they were struggling with their horses were the very things they were sharing with me in conversation. Their personal lives and states of mind affected how they were doing everything. "You can't just teach them methods," he said. "You have to help them become happier people. I know you'd rather just be around horses. But if you care about the horses, then you have to be here for the people."

This sentence has stuck in my head. When I'm tired, overstimulated, in an airport waiting for my next flight to get to a clinic surrounded by hundreds of people, or at social gatherings for networking and connection-building, I often think of this sentence. I do care about people, but I had been preserving myself and my energy and not giving it freely to the people. If I care about the horses, I need to be here for the people.

Over the past few years, I've worked hard to expand my comfort zones. I try to make a conscious effort to be available to people who might need help. I have role models: when I ride with Brent Graef, I see how he is available to people from sunup to sundown. He's sincere about it, and the sincerity makes folks feel comfortable enough to ask questions, try hard things, and make good changes. This is what I want for my students also. Instead of hiding in my trailer for lunch and dinner during a clinic, I've worked on making myself available too.

I'll never be the chatty, extroverted type. I'll never love schmoozing or small talk. In my mind, I balance expanding my comfort zones with staying genuine. My focus will always be on horses and people, but entertaining and just talking to talk isn't part of who I am. At a clinic this year, an older cowboy leaned over the fence and said, "Lady, you're not like the other clinicians. The other guys tell stories. They talk a lot. At least half of the clinic is chatting and telling stories. You don't spend a lot of time talking."

I turned to the participants and asked, "Ladies, what do you think? Do you want me to tell some stories, or do you want to ride?"

"Ride!" they all shouted unanimously. I looked back at the cowboy and shrugged.

Learning to Learn, Not to Follow

In the horse world, as in others, there is a desire for people to group into "camps" and follow someone whose teaching they like. There is nothing wrong with this, until it becomes blind following. People get excited about the ideas of some teacher and start to believe that person, above all others, holds the key to their success.

The truth is there's not much new training information out there. We have learned a ton about equine biomechanics, brains, and care and keeping, but the training ideas many of us use are centuries old. Even if I stumble onto something that works, surely someone before me has thought of it and employed it. I don't take credit for any methods or philosophies I embrace. They aren't unique to me.

Of course, every person makes them their own, and their individual styles affect the results they get. I think of myself as a teacher, and my job is to help other folks understand how to get along with horses to the best of my knowledge and ability. The thing is, both of those things change constantly. What I think of as good for the horse now might not be the same as next year. My interest is not for folks to "follow me" or take my word as gospel, because I may be wrong. My hope is to give people tools to get along better, observe more, and take it from there.

The amount of ego in the horse training industry is baffling when you think about it this way, because the credit belongs to the horses we've learned from along the way and to the pioneers of horse training throughout the centuries whose trial and error we stand on. Aside from the amount of personal work we have put into learning, there is no credit to be had. And as far as skill goes, anyone can have it. The difference between the master and the beginner is only hours of practice and resources available. They can have it too. I am not more special than anyone else, nor is any expert.

Though some folks are more naturally inclined to have good feel, I believe anyone can develop it. So as you're learning, learn from everyone you can. Take what you wouldn't do, what you would do, and what you hope you can someday do, and sort through it. But don't put your teachers on a pedestal. Walk away from anyone who looks down on your skill level. The difference between you and them is only a matter of practice.

The Devil You Don't Know

The relationships we have with our horses often painfully reflect the rest of our lives—whether we avoid conflict or seek it out, whether we are too passive or too aggressive, or whether we fluctuate between the two. It tends to shed light on the good, the bad, and the ugly in a way that can be very uncomfortable.

One thing that I've learned about people, throughout my time as a teacher, is that people try to avoid discomfort and therefore become committed to their regular and routine dysfunction. This is why horse training is so tricky. People have subconscious ways of sabotaging the horse's progress when it gets into territory they aren't familiar with. Even when their regular interactions with their horses are unpleasant, stressful, or even dangerous, the devil you know is better than the devil you don't know. The discomfort of feeling out of their element, learning to behave in new and different ways, or accepting personal responsibility for the dysfunction can be too great for some to bear. It's much easier to work on learning different training methods, and new tricks, rather than deep personal change.

I've often noticed the phenomenon of getting to the heart of the matter when I work with a problem horse without the owner. Things are looking up. The horse is becoming more confident and peaceful. Yet now the client actually becomes less satisfied. I've had clients create contention over seemingly minor issues that didn't exist before and end up taking their horses home. I've had clients sneak back to their old habits (such as feeding treats to the nippy horse) when they think I'm not watching, while resentfully commenting, "It's my horse and I'll do what I please."

These people are not bad people. They're often great people who came to get help and love their horses. But I think it's an important discussion to have. If we don't recognize the disconnect between trying to get to a better place while staying comfortable with dysfunction, we can't help our horses.

The ego is a nasty thing, and we each have ours to deal with. Eckhart Tolle, author and mindfulness teacher, describes the ego as a living entity. I like thinking of it as alive because it helps me understand how otherwise good people can lash out, retreat, or return to dysfunction with so much devotion. The ego wants to live and is being confronted. Having a light shined on it threatens its very existence. It has a sneaky little way of keeping itself strong, and if we aren't aware and open, we may not even realize the cycle of ego keeping us in our bad, unhelpful ways.

This is what I think Ray Hunt meant when he said, "When I see your horse, I see you too." Horses are such amazing teachers because they really show us what's inside of us and offer the unique opportunity to make real changes in our lives.

Empathy

Love is not a sort of rare commodity—everybody has it.
—Alan Watts

Hear me out: I don't believe empathy is unnatural. I believe it is conditioned out of people over the years. When I was a kid, I desperately wanted to be friends with the horses I rode in lessons. When my instructor would scream "KICK HIM," I was torn between not disappointing her and not wanting to harm my friend. She would explain it away: "You have to teach him who's boss," "You can't hurt him, you're too little," "If you don't get him, he will get you!"

Over the years, the harming of horses became more subtle: the kicking and pulling of a beginner gave way to the obsession with a horse's headset and incessant micromanaging with my hands and legs. All of these were led and conditioned repetitively by instructors. If it were up to the little girl 26 years ago, I would have probably kicked and pulled significantly less.

Unlearning these habits was not easy for me. Learning to see from a horse's perspective was hard, too, because I had these responses conditioned into me. Though I have always deeply loved horses and never wanted to harm them, learning more about how they think, move, and see confronted my habits and left me in a strange place in between harsh practices that don't work and ineffective fluff-ery.

Learning to be effective without being harsh and devoid of empathy is a pretty straight shot for someone who hasn't been repetitively conditioned to kick, pull, seesaw, and grind. Even well-meaning, kind people are going to really struggle to not do these things, after the habits have been cemented.

Most children want to ride because they love horses, and inside they know when what they're being asked to do is wrong. Most children look at horses with empathy and care in a way that the adult eye, clouded with conditioned beliefs, goals, traditions, or the burdens of stress, tends to miss. Many of my students are "decompressing" from prior instruction that caused them to go against their deep moral center. As a result, they don't trust their instincts and struggle to connect in meaningful ways with their horse. Their relationship is clouded with fear, doubt, dependence on a trainer, and lack of enjoyment.

There is a part of you that knows you don't want to harm your horse, and knows what is right and what isn't. You know when your horse's eye says he is not ok, even if your instruction has led you to believe he is fine. Trust that little voice—it knows the way back to the innocent enjoyment of a child with a horse.

Imposter Syndrome

Not long ago, I was looking through pictures from a few years ago and realized how many ideas and ways of training I have dropped. Photos of me smiling on tense horses with poor frames. I was proud of my work then, and had worked hard to get there. I didn't know better and was truly doing the best I could. But present me knows better. I wouldn't let myself from two years ago ride my horse today.

I can't tell you how many times I've wondered if I know anything at all, and only know what I don't want to do anymore but don't yet know how to get what I want.

This year has been my most rewarding, wonderful, inspiring year with horses. I've had connections get deeper, horses get more balanced, students smile more and find changes within themselves that make me proud. But I'm sure in a few years I'll look back on my work this year with the same cringe factor that I look back on a few years ago.

My point in all this, friends, is that you are not alone in your concerns, worries, struggles, and fears. "Will I ever meet my goals? Will I ever ride better? Will my horse ever relax, canter, get caught?" I've never met a horseman or -woman worth their salt who doesn't have at least one yearly crisis of wondering what they know, where they've come from, and what they need to know.

It doesn't matter how slow you feel like you're going. It doesn't matter how many mistakes you're making or have made. It doesn't matter whether you lost your temper yesterday or fell off or don't know if you should ever be near a horse again. If you are drawing breath, and you have the desire, you can do it. If you're willing to listen to the horse and settle into the journey for the long haul, you can and will do it. Nobody can walk your journey for you, but there are so many wonderful horses to keep you company along the way.

Riding with Anxiety

I talk a lot about being mentally balanced to help horses. Being able to be in the moment with horses is essential to good horsemanship, but I think it would be wrong to say that you have to be mentally perfect to do well. Folks who have anxiety and such types of issues can often feel like their mental ailments are a burden or disability to their work with horses. Certainly they can be, but if channeled correctly, I believe they can be a tremendous asset. I'll stick to talking about anxiety for the purpose of this article, primarily because, as a lifelong sufferer of anxiety, it's the one I'm most familiar with.

Anxiety can take us out of the moment, overwhelm us with worry and tension, and interfere with our lives. To be a good rider, we need to be able to be in the moment, and to feel for and direct a horse. Sufferers of anxiety are often hypersensitive to their environment. They pick up on every little detail and are aware of things that many people aren't. They can have an upper hand on other folks when it comes to horses because of this sensitivity and ability to empathize with a horse.

So many horses experience chronic fear and stress as well. A person with anxiety has a great advantage, in terms of connecting with a horse, for this reason—they are painfully aware of how burdensome, exhausting, and isolating it can be to be hyper-aware. They understand how small things others might not think much of can trigger panic, and how hard it can be to relax. Because of this, a rider with anxiety can learn to channel their focus into supporting the horse in a way others might not even know the horse needs.

Riding, too, can provide much-needed stability, mindfulness, and a feeling of calm. It might be one of the only places a person with anxiety can feel this way. Someone with anxiety can learn to develop a place of mental stillness in the barn or in the saddle more easily than in other areas of their lives. Because it might have been harder to do this, a person with anxiety can often appreciate and capitalize on this calmness without taking it for granted.

Of course, without good mental care, developing good daily practices, and supportive friends and family, anxiety can make riding exceedingly difficult. For those who are willing and able to work on managing their anxiety, it can give a rider an upper hand that others might not have access to: empathy, sensitivity, and a deep understanding of how to guide a horse toward calm.

Riding with Trauma

I had a lesson recently with a sweet woman who began with an apology: "I'm sorry I don't always learn well, I have some trauma I'm dealing with."

This really struck me, especially for the topic we were discussing: horses in various stages and kinds of physical and mental trauma. We discussed a situation where she had worked with a horse who had behavioral issues, and she felt he was doing much better. Then, during a ride, he came apart and launched her, causing her serious injury.

This is how trauma works: sometimes you are ok, sometimes you aren't. You don't always know what will set off flashbacks and memories, or trigger responses out of your control. Did she miss an important element in training with this horse? Maybe, I have no idea since I'm not her, I'm not the horse, and I wasn't there. But likely it was a traumatized horse, and somehow a trigger was flipped—maybe she could have done something differently, maybe not.

Trauma, unfortunately, is incredibly common in humans. The statistics are troubling: physical and sexual abuse in children are sadly too common (25 out of 1000 children are physically abused, and 1 out of 9 girls and 1 in 53 boys are sexually abused). Physical and sexual abuse in adults are also very common. Illness, injury, abusive relationships, accidents, death, loss, military service and combat, you name it. You most likely know someone who has trauma or PTSD, if you don't have it yourself.

How can trauma benefit our riding? Well, for starters, the obvious: empathy. Horses' behavior is often a cry for help—a signal that things are not ok. Trauma can be anything a horse didn't understand: a first saddling that went poorly, pulling back and breaking a tie, losing a rider as a greenie, or a long stay at the vet hospital. We can't downplay these events just because we understand them—to the horse, they were traumatic.

A person with trauma often knows how it feels to be brushed off, told "It wasn't that bad," "Just live in the moment," "They didn't have bad intentions," "Be glad it wasn't worse," and many other dismissive and unhelpful statements. Similarly, people make comments like this with horses: "Nobody has hit him in years!" "He didn't freak out nine times and on the tenth just lost it for no reason," "He has a good life now after we rescued him, I don't know why he's afraid."

If you've had trauma, you know nice treatment doesn't erase the event that created the trauma or its long-lasting effects and that sometimes you might be ok, and others not. You know how unhelpful it can be to be dismissed, and how easy it might be to stuff it down and no longer show how you feel to keep others comfortable. You know how easy it might be for an explosively fearful animal to go internal, when they aren't allowed to show fear behavior. Your trauma can make you a better rider, a better trainer, and a better human. Because if you have trauma, you know what horses everywhere go through every day.

The Right Path

Finding the right path for me was rewarding, but incredibly uncomfortable. I worked very hard to learn what I knew—but deep down I knew it wasn't working. Horses were scared, mine weren't improving, and I kept running into the same stumbling blocks over and over. I'd fix one problem, create another problem, and have to fix that one.

When I met both of my teachers, what immediately stood out was the peace that surrounded them and every horse they touched. I knew it was right. But that did not make it easier for me to learn. They both said things that were totally contrary to my muscle memory and learned philosophy. I argued with them in my head. "Don't pull!" they said. "I'm not pulling!" I thought defensively. I knew it wasn't right, but letting go was difficult. And I did not yet have the skill to achieve what they asked, so it felt like an absolute mess. I had to let go and trust the process. I saw the end result they had with other horses and knew I wanted it: I had to give up everything I had worked so hard for to get something I'd never had before.

My horses became easier to catch. They wore happier expressions and seemed more peaceful overall. I knew it was right, but I was still struggling with my habits. I wanted to micromanage the front end of the horse, but I knew I had to educate my seat and the horse's hind legs instead. Things got very messy, but when I felt what I could achieve—a straight, happy, loose horse on a loose rein—I was hooked.

Teaching it to my students was even more difficult. "You want me to do what??" "But he's falling into the corners!" "He's just not listening!" "I can't let him get away with that!" Some students quit me—and I can't say I blame them. If I hadn't seen the results myself, I would think I was crazy too. The ones who stuck it out worked so hard, and their horses are more beautiful every day. It's a pleasure for me to see beautiful, strong, confident, and happy horses, and I sure hope those riders are proud of their work!

When the path feels right, you know it inside. But that doesn't mean it will be easy. I had to fight against every habit my hands and legs were trained to do for years. I had to give up everything I'd learned to get here: It doesn't work if you just dabble in it. You have to live it. I'm so grateful my teachers didn't give up on me, teaching me the same lesson each time for years until I got it. I'm still working on myself, but now I am dedicated to this path. I see the way my horses look and feel, and there is no turning back.

Toddlers and Horses

It's been said that good horsemanship is the art of mastering not the horse, but your own body and mind. In my younger training days, I could get a little dogmatic or judgmental about people's struggle to be patient with horses—ugly emotions coming out at the trailer or in a ride were hard for me to understand sometimes. I don't pretend to be perfect. I practice at being patient because it serves me (for example, not getting bucked off).

When my daughter was born, things got a lot messier. My husband worked, and I was riding six to eight horses a day with an infant and two dogs. I was sleep-deprived, the dogs were hyper because they weren't getting as much attention and exercise as they were used to pre-baby, and I suddenly found myself understanding how someone could be less patient.

(Read: I was less patient.)

I was tossed into a world of torturous sleep deprivation, back pain, and a wobbly core after what felt like a nine-year pregnancy. I was suffering from the poor eating habits that accompany just getting by and dealing with un-wanted parenting advice and rude comments from strangers, while learn-ing to balance my workload with the needs of a new and helpless person. It was a lot.

Every baby phase has its wonderful parts and parts you hope will pass soon. Josie is a toddler now, almost two. She's strong, vibrant, beautiful, and very much testing boundaries. There are no's that are absolutely essen-tial to her safety ("Don't touch the electric fence") and no's that are really sometimes a battle best avoided ("Maybe it's not the end of the world if you relocate all the hoof picks or draw on the wall").

I love riding, and I love my daughter. I want to be the best I can be with both. And I'm incredibly grateful for so many opportunities in my life to practice being mindful, being patient, being empathetic, and being aware. I'll take all the help I can get, even if it is Patience Bootcamp, run by a tiny, but adorable, dictator and all her four-legged friends.

Advice for Up-and-Coming Women

While being interviewed for a podcast, the interviewer asked me what advice I had for up-and-coming horsewomen. I gave her my answer, but once the interview was over, I really got to thinking.

My advice to young women is to be yourself. To be an example of what you want the horse world to be, not to fit into what it accepts and rewards. To make this change, you have to be brave enough to be vulnerable, to be soft, to be honest. Everyone advises hard work, and it's true, you shouldn't be afraid of hard work. But you have to have the gumption to say no, to walk away from places and people who take advantage or do harm. That is far harder than putting your head down and working more.

The truth is that opportunities don't always come to people who work hard and are respectful. Sometimes you get buried under a mountain of more work, and less respect. So work hard, but protect yourself. Say no, take a day off, take care of your body.

Don't compete with others; lift them up. Encourage your peers, even if—and especially if— you think they're on the wrong path. You never know what an outstretched hand can do for someone. There is plenty of success available for everyone. Don't elbow your peers out of the way.

Young women, you don't have to be as good as the men in our field. You have to be the best you: use your strengths to interact with horses in the most authentic, real way that you can. You will always fail at trying to be as tough, as charismatic, as showboating, or as strong as the men our industry has put on a pedestal are. And you don't want to be brash, rude, and cold like many of the women who have made it to higher positions. Be yourself—it will take guts, but there's never been a better time to do it. The horse world is changing for the better. There is a place for you, you are needed, you are wanted.

Defense Mechanisms

"You use humor as a defense mechanism," my therapist said. "You made me laugh with your story, but it's actually very sad."

The story I had just conveyed was about an internship I'd had years ago with a particularly difficult-natured and very well-known teacher. I had about 22 feet of lead rope and a wild horse on the other end. She had yelled at me for days over my sloppy coiling of this rope, and the more she yelled, the more tense I got. Finally, my brain completely shut down until I couldn't remember how to even hold a lead rope. One of the horses we were working with had bolted, and the horse was spinning circles around me while my teacher yelled at me over my sloppy coils. I had described the situation laughingly, saying I was "wrapped up like a mummy."

I don't cry much in public, and in fact, I make it my personal goal in life to not cry in front of people. But this teacher made me cry just about every day, in front of my friends and a camera crew. Telling the story made me laugh, until my therapist pointed that out. Suddenly the story hurt, and the humiliation, frustration, and pain came flooding back. When I left this internship, I felt like quitting riding altogether and didn't feel like I could even lead a horse, let alone ride one.

The day after this therapy session I was scheduled to have a private lesson with Mark Rashid. I was still feeling very raw from the session, feeling as if someone had taken my skin off and the sensitive jelly beneath was exposed. I could feel myself getting nervous when I walked into the arena with my training horse and saw a crowd of auditors. Suddenly I was filled with flashbacks of gawking people watching me cry while I got yelled at. Internships, jobs, clinics: they often went the same. A group of people watches a teacher ridicule me publicly for my mistakes. The whispers of the crowd, the anxious horse, the yelling teacher would send me into sensory overload, and I couldn't think or perform basic tasks. I choked the memory down and did my best to focus.

After a few minutes of groundwork, Mark said, "Your lead rope is a little short for this exercise. Let's use the 22-footer I have here." Gulp. The lead rope must have been made of lead, because the weight of it in my hands was matched only by the weight of my dread. A whole crowd was watching me fumble with my lead rope. I doubted Mark would yell at me, but the public can be cruel, and they remember your mistakes for years to come. I still hear about a bad ride I had at a stuffy dressage clinic years ago, and the sting of the critique from the crowd still rises when I'm in a clinic situation.

We worked on ground driving for a bit, Mark gave me some suggestions, and I braced myself for the inevitable badness to come. "You're doing a great job handling that rope," Mark said. I felt a twinge inside that I struggled to push down. The dam was bursting, and suddenly a flood of emotions were about to be unleashed. Years of insecurity, anxiety, criticism, fear of learning, fear of performing in public, fear of not being good enough. Beneath all of that, hidden away, a deep desire to be seen and validated. All my old junk was, over the years, tied up in neat little knots, stuffed down and held together with humor as the glue: people like you better if you laugh, and they can't make fun of you if you make fun of yourself first. If you tell the story in a humorous way, you can be truthful, be hurting, without drawing sympathy or pity. It's just much more comfortable that way.

Mark didn't insult me. He just kept validating me. He gave me tools and suggestions while telling me I was doing great. My therapist would say we are comfortable with what we know, even if it's bad for us. My discomfort at being treated like a human being worthy of respect in a clinic was overwhelming, and I at that moment totally understood what the mare I was handling experienced with me for months: complete suspicion at the nice display and waiting it out for the other shoe to drop.

Kyber, the mustang I had with me that day, had come to me without a shred of trust in people, incredibly difficult to handle. She had been ridden and described as "very dull" by her former trainer. Once she was purchased, she was unable to be caught and extremely wary. When I picked her up for training, she had been feral in her large field for several years. A vet had darted her with sedative multiple times in hopes of allowing us to catch her, and still she wasn't approachable.

I had told Kyber with the way I was catching her that it would not be like she knew or expected. She was like the Great Stone Horse, not breathing, and expected to be cornered to be caught. I worked on getting her to draw in, to relax, and to feel like she had some room to make decisions. Sometimes she would relax so much she'd yawn, stretch, and even lie down next to me. Other times it was like I'd hit a switch by accident somewhere and she'd bolt.

By the time of the clinic, I'd had her for five months. She rested her nose on my arm while I talked to Mark, checked in with me, breathed on my neck. She trusted me, and that was a tremendous honor. That trust was built, I felt, on being the same person every day for months. It wasn't built on any magical horse whispering, or technique. It was just as simple as being consistent in my approach, waiting for her, listening to her, and letting her speak. Not playing nice only to turn around and get impatient or too firm.

The trouble I'd had with people was the same as Kyber. People acted nice to start with, to draw you in. They told you what you wanted to hear, gave you nuggets of hope—"You're so talented, you should be my student. You'll go far!" Then they were screaming at you, and all the qualities that they praised in you at the beginning were laid out and dissected on the table. The sensitivity you possess was a major flaw, your curiosity, your willingness to watch and ask questions: all of those things got you in trouble. People value you for your work ethic but resent your need for respect, for space, for time to think. So you shut down, you run away, or you do both.

Unlike people, horses make intelligent investments in themselves: if people aren't trustworthy, they run away and don't let themselves be caught. Unless someone can prove they are not a threat, horses continue their cycle of self-defense. People, like myself, continue seeking out the same scenario that hurt us. For whatever insane reason, I continued actually paying people to denigrate me publicly. Or working for people who did so. I subconsciously went out of my way to end up in scenarios where I was not safe, mentally or physically.

Horses like to feel good. If you can show them how to relax and find mental and physical well-being, they will choose it and stay there. Lesser beings like the human have to go to therapy, find out why they continue acting in self-destructive cycles, and cry over a compliment. It's what Mark talks about constantly—good horsemanship isn't about technique, or skill, or physical strength, though those can help. It's about finding internal softness to present to a horse, something to offer them that's real, comforting, and safe. If the inside of a person can get right, any horse they meet, in time, can get right too.

Elbows

My teacher says, "Weight your elbow! It belongs beside your waist, and everything hinges from there." She says the balance in everything we do comes from your core, in hand or in the saddle, and you don't lift your elbow away for leverage.

I need surgery on my elbow. I have a compressed nerve that makes my entire arm numb, as the result of an old injury. A few years back, I came off a mustang and tore the tendons in my arm. It healed painfully slowly and eventually led to nerve problems. When she says, "Flutter your whip, don't smack with it!" I'm taking a shot in the dark—I fiddle around until she seems happy. I can't feel my hand, I don't know what my hand is doing to the whip. It's like I'm wearing someone else's arm and watching it work without me. I don't know where my elbow is, but I am learning to feel that when my core is in center, my elbow is too.

Why did I ride that horse years ago? I didn't need to, even though my old boss threatened me with no pay. I could have said no, but I caved. I was afraid of the horse, but more afraid of upsetting my boss. But what's an upset person matter when your arm is in a sling? What's a little disapproval in comparison to a spill, years of chronic pain, an arm that doesn't function? What's one measly check out of months of lost income? What's one ride out of years of lost confidence?

I used to ride with locked elbows. I kept my arms straight ahead of me and my front body closed off. I rode defensively. I rode lots of bronc-y colts and snorty horses, until one dumped me badly enough to shake my confidence. My self-esteem was wrapped up in what movements I could ride out. With torn tendons in my arm, I didn't have the strength in my hand to hold on anymore. The mechanism I had relied on was taken away. I saw a video once explaining posture and a person's emotional state, which described how closing the front body reflected a person in a state of emotional protection and insecurity. I was living life defensively.

My teacher says that riding in balance and making horses in balance eliminates the need for riding defensively. If the back is supple, there is no need to protect yourself. That requires that I let go of my defensiveness and open my front body—to really trust. When I stay open, relaxed, and swing with the horse, my hands don't pull, and my elbow, with its pins and needles, prickly hot yet somehow numb-feeling, stays in its place. I create a stable balance that the horse can follow, and if I don't defend myself against them, they don't need to defend themselves against me.

It amazes me how my elbow, when it holds its ground, has enough swing in it to give without letting go of its balance; it isn't pulled forward by the horse, but it isn't a rock that braces against the horse either. I guess that's the balance I'm learning—to be strong in my own position, but with that strength comes just enough flexibility to not create resistance. If it takes a grumpy nerve in my elbow to teach me that, then so be it. I am grateful for my elbow.

You Are Your Best Teacher

Over the years, I've studied and worked as an intern under many great trainers. I've studied hard and tried my best to please my teachers. But teachers aren't always right. And the person giving instruction on the ground, no matter how well-meaning, does not have to bear the consequence of accident or injury. You do.

I often say to my students, "What I am telling you is just my interpretation of what I see that your horse needs." That means I could be wrong.

Or, it could mean that what I would choose to do at that moment may not be right for you. Here's something else I've learned: as students, we need to keep one ear on the instruction and one ear on what's going on more internally. For example, we have to assess our ability, assess our confidence level in the moment, and assess our understanding of the instruction. There are many ways to work at something. While there are merits to pushing our boundaries and our comfort levels, listening to our gut is an important lesson and one to always keep in mind during the educational process.

I know this personally from a bit of recent hindsight. These past few years of trial, growth, and a handful of injuries have taught me a lot about rushing, about riding green horses before I or they are ready, and about working on a set schedule. While being laid up, I've had plenty of time to think about what this all means. The phase of my life called "being a good student" is over. "Being brave" is done too. The new phase of my life is called "listening to my gut and being smart," and it has just begun. Now, my interest is learning from my own instinct. I throw out pressures to ride a certain way or to get horses going at any rate other than the horse's and mine.

It's my career, my well-being, and my conscience on the line. I wave off memories of every time I've been told to "grow a pair"; every time I've heard "Haven't you ridden him yet?"; every time I have had something to prove; every time I cheapened my horsemanship and ignored what the horse needed and was telling me, just to get a job done or keep a client.

Now, the only one pushing me is myself and my horse. The horse can trust my investment in a good outcome in any given hour, day, or month. I encourage you to do the same. Take all teaching with a grain of salt. Be a Horse Pleaser and a Conscience Pleaser, not a People Pleaser. Because after all, it's only money and it's only time. What do you have without your health, your peace of mind, and your relationship with your horse?

Are You a Leader or a Partner?

When I teach, I often ask students for their goals. Most people say they want a good relationship with their horse and a better partnership. As the lesson goes on, their frustrating problems creep up and we get down to the nitty-gritty, dealing with what happens when things don't go the way they want. I see fighting, temper flare-ups, frustration, name-calling, and the use of force—and that's just on the human side.

From our first encounter, we're taught that we're supposed to be the horse's leader. Whether it's worded "Show 'em who's boss" or "Be the leader," the idea is similar. The human calls the shots and the horse obeys. But many of the people looking to be the horse's leader lack a real understanding of what the horse actually needs, or the education and timing to provide it. It's like taking a kindergarten class and demanding you be the teacher of that class at the same time. You're getting your bearings about you, learning your ABCs, but demanding the other kids listen to you while you teach them your half-learned alphabet song.

Sometimes in my lessons, the rider has totally misinterpreted the situation that frustrated her in the first place. For example, she thinks the horse is not listening to her when he won't go, but actually the rider's hands are blocking the horse from going. In that case, the horse was listening, and the rider was leading. But no points are scored in the relationship department. Or, the rider wants to lead, but doesn't really have an idea of what she wants. Years ago, I had a client who was frustrated by her horse wandering off the trail and getting too close to the other horses on a trail ride. When I asked what she had planned to do about it, she said, "Well, I don't really steer, I just try to enjoy the ride." How can you be a leader if you don't provide input for the lead?

If it's a partnership you want, it isn't all about calling the shots. In a good partnership, there is give-and-take. Sometimes I lead the horse, sometimes I follow. To me, it's an artful and delicate dance, where I try not to let the horse take over, but I listen to the horse and go with their needs in their time.

I think of good riding as teaching. When I teach lessons, I don't demand a compliant response from my students. I don't apply more pressure when they don't comply. This type of relationship doesn't interest me because it doesn't actually teach. Sure, I can get the satisfaction of having my ego stroked, but I didn't create any real learning. What I want out of our student-teacher relationship is a thoughtful, engaged dialogue. I offer feedback, direction, and exercises to get to where the student wants to go. In turn, the student needs to engage, think, experiment, and essentially learn to feel their horse and try things because they understand the concepts, not just because I instructed them.

When I work with young or troubled horses, there is leading in the sense that I offer direction and guidance. But it isn't all about doing what I want. It's about creating that same dialogue—a safe space where they're free to try, to learn, and to let down enough for us to be on the same page. A young horse might offer to canter because they feel good. If I shut her down because it isn't what I wanted, because I have to be the "leader," I take away from our relationship. I've just proven to this horse that her efforts, her exuberance, her willingness is not appreciated. And what becomes of that effort later on when I ask for a canter, after I have shut down the horse's willingness to go forward?

Leadership means guiding—it doesn't just mean making the horse do what you want, when you want it. If you can't guide, what does the horse have to follow? Frustrations can arise because the horse won't do what you want, and she seems to take over. But it's natural for a horse to take over when there isn't enough guidance, or the guidance is poor or conflicts with the horse's self-interest, especially as it concerns the horse's security. A horse wants to feel secure and balanced. If you can't provide that, he will look elsewhere. He'll whinny or tune out, maybe drag you to the gate or try to go back to the barn. Do we have something worth listening to?

I don't want a robot. I want a thinking, engaged partner. And a partner is someone who has input. They have some say in how things go. Need things to move slower? You got it, partner. Scared? I got your back. Frustrated? I'll break it down for you.

Mindful Beginners

One of the most common and damaging times for rider education starts, unfortunately, at the outset. Beginner-level school horses are often gentle but uneducated, and beginner instructors often have the least amount of experience. This creates lasting and unfortunate damage to riders and horses.

There is a prevalent idea in the horse world that an instructor of beginner riders is less skilled, and that a lesson horse suitable for a beginner rider needs to be gentle but not necessarily educated. People as well often look down on the beginner horse and teacher, as if their job is less difficult and less valuable. Instructors find themselves wanting to move beyond teaching beginners as soon as they get enough experience. Beginners also tend to feel apologetic for their limited skill set, often describing their experience and ability in self-deprecating ways.

I got my start as a teacher with beginner lessons, and I enjoyed them. But even as I learn more and appreciate the basics, I still love teaching beginners, maybe even more than I did at first. I find myself giving better descriptions of the basic elements. In turn, my students have better understanding and excel much faster than they used to. I love to teach beginners the basics of expression, biomechanics, movement, and horsemanship. With an open mind and fresh perspective, they are often incredibly receptive to this information. It can be so rewarding. Some of the best riders I've met were less experienced, at least at first.

With more experienced riders, teaching the basics can feel more difficult. They have ingrained habits that can be hard to break, and they carry a sense of pride in their ability. When tune-ups to their basics are needed, it can be hard on their self-esteem.

Contrary to conventional wisdom, a new rider can get a great start with knowledgeable instructors and horses who are not just gentle but well educated. They can get expert direction in the foundational pieces that will carry on through their riding careers. With an educated horse, beginners get a feel for the more finessed movements in riding. An instructor who has a finely tuned eye and experience teaching riders of all levels can set up a beginner for the stepping-stones to move beyond rudimentary riding skills.

Meanwhile, an inexperienced instructor teaching a new rider can shortchange the beginner's learning experience. Learning to ride with the kick-and-pull mechanics as a foundation is tough to fix later. Riders who've spent hours cementing the muscle memory of pulling and kicking to maneuver the horse, or poor or incorrect muscle memory for their riding position, will struggle to undo it later. Having an instructor with a keen eye for the basics of horsemanship and rider mechanics from the get-go will set the rider up for better riding sooner. This kind of instructor can nurture a rider to move past the kick-and-pull phase to more quickly access a higher level of sensitivity and feel, and to develop these abilities instead of restricting them by encouraging mindless riding.

When I see a beginner with a disinterested instructor, a student riding endless laps on a stiff, gold-hearted horse, hearing the occasional directive to kick more, I feel sad for the horse world. The natural empathy and sensitivity of that rider—which likely drew them to horses in the first place—is systematically trained out with mindless directives. This beginner doesn't get to experience fluidity of motion, connection, harmony, or suppleness. If she doesn't know these things exist, she is fated to create more disconnected partnerships throughout their riding life. The cycle of stiff horses and stiff, unfeeling riders is perpetuated by mindless instruction that emphasizes control over feeling and connection. What does it take to break the cycle?

- Better instruction for beginners and better-educated horses
- More time learning the ins and outs of horsemanship, horse psychology, movement, and care
- Less focus on getting to shows or moving up the levels
- More time on the lunge line, getting confident in following the horse's movement
- Less time learning to control the horse before understanding the horse
- Fewer circles and laps around the arena
- More time observing, listening, and thinking

Beginner students taught optimally have a much better chance at getting along with horses, hopefully, staying with riding long-term, and eventually becoming teachers of mindful horsemanship themselves someday.

The Enemy of Feel

The enemy of feel is being in a hurry. I know this to be true, but, while I'm waiting for my horse to have his breakthrough, I have six other training horses left to ride, a baby crying in the corner, a dog barking at a horse, and the phone ringing.

Bill Dorrance often talked about not minding the wait. Tom Dorrance frequently said, "Even if you miss your lunch . . . wait." Ray Hunt said, "It takes the time it takes." So how do you maintain a calm, patient composure and keep offering a good feel for the horse when you don't have all day to wait? My life as of late has been an ongoing experiment in this very subject. Here are some rules I've found that make all the difference, in order of importance.

1. **Center yourself.** If you haven't done this, do not pass go, do not collect $200. Go back inside and start again. Centering yourself doesn't mean the baby is quiet and the dog isn't barking; it means you have found an internal place of acceptance where you can deal with exactly what is, not what you wanted it to be. Deep breaths are very helpful. I have a meditation app on my phone because I like the five-minute guided meditations—then I'm ready to start.

2. **Pick one thing to work on.** Make it simple, and if you're limited on time, make it extremely simple. Set it up so the horse comes out of this session successful. If you know that riding down by the scary end of the arena is always an issue, but you only have a half hour, ride somewhere easy. Do not pick a fight—I repeat, do not pick a fight.

3. **Leave it alone.** It may sound counterintuitive, but if you make a nice change, give them a long break. Yes, I know you're running out of time, and you don't think you have time to stand and watch them relax and mull over the lesson, but the research shows this very act of "doing nothing" after a small success accelerates learning. Slow down faster to get there sooner. Your future sessions will really show your effort off.

4. **Backtrack.** If things aren't working out, don't end your session feeling upset about what isn't working. Go do something you both can do. Do not drill. Go back to step number one if you feel your frustration level rising.

5. **Do some calisthenics—it never hurts!** If you only have 15 minutes, simple balancing and loosening exercises, even in hand, can make a significant difference in a horse's mental and physical well-being.

6. **Reward plenty, reward often, reward generously.** This can be with breaks, internal softening, some nice rubs, whatever. But make it feel good to the horse. Please don't slap the bejesus out of their necks—nobody likes that.

7. **End on a good note.** End on a good note. End on a good note . . . Leave them feeling better than you found them. End on a good note!!

Toxic Trainers

Over the years, I've had many (too many—I'm a slow learner, it seems) experiences with teachers and employers who damage your self-esteem and make you feel two inches tall.

I'm sure it's a thing for all disciplines, but the horsemanship world seems to be filled with braggarts and arrogant people who criticize, ridicule, and holler. Their client base is largely middle-aged women, lacking in self-esteem, who take their emotional lashings as if they deserve it. It seems with a cowboy hat and false sense of confidence, they can convince the world that they are masterful, and that their students don't possess the skill to ever get close to their ability.

Over the past decade, my confidence has plummeted repeatedly after each interaction with these kinds of teachers. Clinicians who publicly ridicule you for asking a question. Teachers who make you question why you call yourself a professional for not doing things their way. People who make you feel like a coward for not wanting to ride beyond your or the horse's ability. Many times I nearly quit teaching and riding professionally, wanting to hide in a hole instead.

I know I'm not alone in this, as every one of my professional peers has similar stories, and many of my students have had the same experience with teachers. So I feel compelled to put together a list of what a good teacher should be, and to repeat again and again, that a true horseman has compassion. A true horseman can't be one way with people and another with horses. I know people often say, "He's a little tough around the edges with people, but he's a great hand." Well, having seen enough of these people behind the scenes, when no one of import is watching, I can say with confidence: if they are rude to people, they're guaranteed to be critical, harsh, and rude to horses too—just maybe not when the crowd is watching. So what makes a good teacher?

- Good teachers won't ridicule you publicly.
- They won't make you do something that goes against your moral center. If you feel that it's wrong and harmful to your horse, it probably is.
- They won't intentionally scare you. They may push your boundaries a little, and they may ask you to do things you can't do, but they shouldn't put you in danger.
- They won't criticize you personally. While it's true that horsemanship and life go hand in hand, personal criticism is not the same as touching a deep nerve that requires our attention.
- They won't scream, yell, and lose emotional control. If you see this, run the other way.
- Good teachers can be hard on you, soft on you, loud, or quiet. But they care about you and your progress. Here are some additional qualities you can expect to find in good teachers:
- They should listen to your concerns and, if needed, explain themselves differently. They may be right. You may be right. If they are

secure in their belief, they will be willing to explain.

- They should believe in you and give praise, even if mixed in with constructive criticism.

- They should care about all horses—even the poorly bred ones, the heavy ones, the dull ones, the ruined ones, the spoiled ones, the nervous ones. They should want the best for your horse and not disparage them.

- They should be honest with you. Sometimes the truth will hurt, but if they care about you, they will be willing to make themselves uncomfortable to tell you the truth so you can succeed.

Right now, after a decade of trial and error, huge drops in confidence, and coming back to try again, I feel extremely grateful to have two mentors that care about my progress, my horses, and me. Both are kind to people and horses across the board, rain or shine, expensive horse or cheap horse, talented rider or poor rider. It makes all the difference.

Tips and Tricks

People very frequently ask me for advice I put in the "tips and tricks" category. How do I stop a bolting horse? What do I do when he bucks? What's the best way to stop him from spooking? What are a few easy exercises to develop a deep, trusting relationship? What's the best spaghetti stick and noodle desensitization kit to buy? (Just made the last one up 'cause I crack myself up.)

The truth is I can't answer any of those questions, except with this: fix everything. From top to bottom—fix the basics, fix the relationship, ride better, look at the things contributing to this problem and fix or eliminate them, listen to your horse, and don't ride them until they're good and prepared. If things fall apart, get off and fix the basics again.

Immerse yourself in their world. What do they need? What do they lack? How does their body feel? How do they react when you come around, when you ask them for something? What is their habituated response? What do their footfalls sound like—are they rushed, hurried, heavy? Or are they soft, rhythmic, steady? In the packaged-up, fast-food horseman-ship world of three-minute attention spans and viral YouTube videos, it's an unpopular answer to say, look at yourself, and look at the whole picture. Study, think, try.

So many horses are sorely lacking in basic understanding or prepara-tion, just doing the best they can with scared riders. A horse will be con-stantly in a state of self-preservation until their needs are met—they need a happy herd, movement, physical and mental balance, well-fitting tack, proper preparation, and information presented in a way they can under-stand. Until they have those things, they will be looking to the barn, the gate, the other horses for comfort, and you will be stuck in a fix-it mindset. The only real change is done systematically—look to the whole picture, not just the symptoms.

There is no harm that will ever come to you from learning to ride bet-ter and from working on the basics. In fact, I'd say the other way has some pretty high risk.

Nature Is Cruel, but We Don't Have to Be

Sometimes people say things like "They kick and bite each other all the time! Nothing I do with my 140 lb. body can hurt them," or "I'm using the natural hierarchy by being alpha." Let's dissect some of that for a minute.

It's completely natural for horses to kick and bite each other. It's com-pletely natural for this to happen when competing over resources, and it's natural for these resources to be scarce. Nature lets horses starve to death slowly. It lets them get injured and die. Nature makes her share of flowers, and she makes her share of toxins.

I once was with a woman in her field when a horse approached her too closely. Before I could even register what happened, she kicked it right in the chin. I asked her why she did that, and she said, "I'm letting him know who's boss!" If we decide to play that game, we have to understand the risk. If a horse kicks another, and the receiver of the kick retaliates, they have the same equipment to engage in that sort of competition. It's true, that lady in her 110 lb. body doesn't pack nearly as much power as the horse. So, if he had decided to retaliate, she would have been in some big trouble. Training through domination works until it doesn't—a lot of horses come to my barn because they have realized how strong they are, and how strong people are not.

Aside from the fact that domination in herd hierarchies has largely been debunked (see the "Resources" page for a link to research on that), a small person CAN cause pain to a horse. Look at the equipment we have to create fear, pain, and control. Chains, twitches, whips, bits, flags. Of course, not all of these are bad and have to be used to create pain, but most training methods rely on some degree of fear or pain to keep control. So yes, the small old lady absolutely can cause pain and can create learned helplessness, stress, and fear in her herd.

Lastly, we have big, supposedly superior human brains. We've studied horses, we understand their minds, and we can do better. We can train ethically for the same reason we wouldn't let our horses starve or die of preventable diseases. Horses are extremely forgiving, willing creatures. Regardless of the fact that they can be deadly, they are largely peace-seeking animals. They avoid conflict when possible. Horses that create or seek conflict are usually restricted for space, movement, resources, or have human problems. We can and should do better than to rely on fear or pain to work with horses. We have so much information at our fingertips, to not use it is simply not right. As Temple Grandin says, "Nature is cruel, but we don't have to be."

Calm Enough to Help Your Horse

I don't know who needs to hear this, but breaking things down into smaller steps where you and your horse can succeed without fear is NOT cheating, and that progress you're making is still totally valid. You want to get down and walk? Get down and walk. You want company on your first trail ride? Get some company. You want to make sure they investigate the scary things before you ride by them? By all means do it.

If I could eliminate one aspect of equestrian culture, it would be the "hospital or back on" mentality. This is coming from someone who deals with scared horses and people daily. This mentality is not producing better riders and more confident horses: it's pumping out more tense, clutching riders who can't direct and scared horses than it ever fixed.

I don't care if you walk until you're ready. I don't care if you get down. What I do care about is that you advocate for yourself and your horse. If you're scared, you aren't helping your horse. And that doesn't help you, me, or the horse.

The Things We Miss in Our World of Words

We humans like to chatter. In the beginning of a lesson, we like to tell our story. We like to make up stories for the horse, talk about the personality we've made up for him, how we think he feels about things, and what he likes and dislikes. We attach human values and emotions to their behavior and responses, and as such, are pulled further away from them and from effective communication with them.

Horses live in a sensory world. They rely on sight, touch, taste, smell, and sound to get through their world. When we ride, the first sensation they feel is our weight shifting on their back. Unaware of our own physical bodies and the meaning our every move has to a horse, we rely heavily on our hands and our voices, and when a horse doesn't respond how we'd planned, we add judgement: "He's dull," "He's disrespectful," "He doesn't want to work," "He needs more leg, spur, inside rein, whatever."

The reality might be, in fact, that none of these things were true, and we were so busy not feeling our bodies and attaching judgement with our busy mouths and minds that we neglected to feel the horse or even listen to his response. I often find myself in a lesson going around with a student about why the horse did something. For example, if a horse pulls to the gate, the student says, "He's mad at me because I was late with his feed, that's why he doesn't want to work." But the answer might simply be that the rider was leaning in that direction and neglected to guide the horse.

The major problem with this, aside from it being inaccurate and anthropomorphic, is that it removes us from the moment and robs us of the ability to actually guide. It forces us into a perpetual pattern of correcting, and with that comes complaining about the horse's behavior. Being in the moment, being out of our heads, actually FEELING and listening to the horse, step-by-step, from the moment we catch them to the moment we turn them loose, allows us to guide, communicate back and forth, and avoid problems in the first place.

We are so used to being in the world of words, we miss what horses have to say: they are sensory beings, quietly communicating with every step, and if you're too busy talking, you miss important messages. For just one ride, I challenge you to listen. See how it feels. You may find your horse is entirely different from the story you tell about him.

Praise without Conditions

I notice something interesting when I teach people, especially women. When I pay attention to improvements and make a big deal of them, many people are often immediately suspicious. The conversation might go something like this:

Me: "You rode that circle very nicely!"

Student: "Well, I still didn't get a good rhythm, my right leg is still too tight, and my horse didn't bend well."

Me: "Ok, but it still is a really nice improvement."

Student: "Well, it could be better."

It sometimes seems that our brains are committed to focusing on the negative aspects of our work, that we aren't allowed to be proud of our improvements. When I ask my students to tell me something they did well, they often look visibly uncomfortable, and if they can come up with something, they add conditions to it. "I got better at x, BUT I still didn't do y and z." I tell them often that a successful moment doesn't need to be described with conditions. You can be aware of what needs improvement without needing to beat yourself over the head with it.

I also think people can get accustomed to the authoritarian-type teacher who just hollers every failure at you, until you accept that you are never going to be as good as them. So a teacher who compliments their improvement and draws on their strengths arouses suspicion—maybe the teacher doesn't know anything if they think I'm good. The thing is, I would never in a million years teach a horse the way some people have become used to being taught. Hanging your failures over your head puts too much emphasis on your shortcomings. Yes, I can see what your leg is doing, but we'll get to that. One thing at a time.

When you ride with a laundry list of your own faults, you don't reward yourself or notice your accomplishments—and you don't notice the horse's either. You can't help it. You think you're being hard on yourself, but you're hard on the horse too. You are allowed to be proud of your improvements. In fact, I highly recommend it.

Confrontation

When I started training, I think I was overly confrontational with my horses. Then, for a while, I avoided it like the plague. Both situations created unbalanced, unhappy horses.

Confrontation is part of life, but we can do it peacefully. If I have a horse kicking at me, pawing at me, or pushing on me, a confrontation is inevitable in some way if we're going to get through that spot. But it doesn't have to be emotional on my end, and it doesn't have to be violent. It isn't personal, and if I look at it as an opportunity to help my horse, it can actually be a really great moment for us to get together. It may be just as simple as making a boundary clear, quietly but firmly. Sometimes problem horses end up being the best saddle horses for this reason—so many opportunities to create a better relationship, better understanding, and better basics.

Confrontation with people is such an art form, and far more complicated. It's bound to happen. It can't be avoided (or at least, it shouldn't be, for a healthy life). You don't have to go picking fights, but communication is everything. People don't often read each other's body language and respond, and we carry lots of ideas, notions, and baggage into the situation that make things far muddier. Was that person rude, or am I just overly sensitive to criticism? Did they say what they really meant or what they thought we wanted to hear? Were they deflecting, lying, trying to avoid something? Humans are not as honest with their feelings as horses are.

A funny example of the importance of communication: One night my husband asked me to hand him a pen while sitting at the kitchen counter. I handed it to him, and we went about our business. Then he asked me for a book, and I handed it to him, and we went on about our business. Some time passed and he asked, "Are you ok?" I looked at him quizzically. "Of course, why?" He replied, "Both times I asked you to hand me something I had my hand open, and you put the thing next to my hand, not in it. Did I upset you?" I explained that I hadn't meant to do that, that I had a splitting headache and hadn't even noticed. We both laughed, I got some ibuprofen, and life was good.

But imagine if he didn't ask me and went on all night thinking I was upset. I would have noticed him acting funny, and maybe gotten anxious, and started avoiding him or acting differently in some way. The two of us could have easily reacted based on our past experiences: him behaving from knowing his partners are always mad at him, me behaving like my partners are always cold and detached. Then our entire night would have been uncomfortable, and it would have all been avoidable with a simple conversation.

Horses can teach us to be better communicators. They can teach us to keep our emotions balanced when having these conversations. They can teach us to read expressions better, to not seek out or avoid conflicts but to deal with them in a healthy way when they do come up. This is the journey horses have taken me on: improving my life through deepened understanding of myself, and for that I am very grateful. I am by no means good at any of this, but thanks to horses, I'm trying to become aware. Because how we are in our day-to-day lives will show up with horses—guaranteed.

Fun

Are you having fun? Not many people use horses for a living anymore. That means that riding and being with horses is a hobby done in our free time. This should free us up to have some fun with it!

So many people I meet are very obviously not having fun. They are frustrated, afraid, over-horsed, shelling out an arm and a leg for their hobby, and seeming to not get enjoyment out of it. Maybe they have a trainer who stresses them out or is harsh and driving. Maybe their boarding barn is full of drama. Maybe the horse is fearful, forward, athletic, young, and they might do better with a confident, quiet older horse.

So are you having fun? You're supposed to be—there may be moments of fear while you work through expanding your comfort zone, but not everlasting dread. There may be moments of frustration while you work through concepts that are new and hard, or when you run into roadblocks, but not frustration overall. Just as a horse needs the right environment of security to learn, people need security to learn as well. So if you aren't having fun, what needs to change?

Maybe you have the wrong horse for you—nothing wrong with that. You don't have to ride all kinds of horses. Maybe you have the wrong trainer. The yelling kind or the overly forceful kind can zap the fun out of anybody's riding. Maybe you don't have a trainer and could benefit from some instruction and help. Maybe your attitude needs a makeover. Maybe your expectations need tweaking. It could be a little of all of these things, some of them, or something completely different. Either way, it's important to remember riding is for fun, so if you aren't having any, something needs to change.

Got Guilt?

Got guilt? Me too. The more I learn, the better things go with my horses. But I can't help thinking back on some of the ways I worked with my horses, some of the big things I missed, some of the ways I failed them. I feel guilty. It's something I hear a lot while teaching: "I just didn't know better." It's true, we don't know what we don't know.

There is nothing we can do to change the past. And just like looking back on history, we can't judge people of the past (including ourselves) for what they did not know. We do the best we can until we know better, and then we change, adapt, and do better.

I try to pay it forward to every horse and rider I see. I try to direct riders onto better habits than I had because I know the damage those habits cause. I try to show a little more grace to people who are lost and judge them less. If they seem to be totally on the wrong path, I try to remember that I used to have absolute certainty I was on the right path, and it was others who were wrong. I try to show more understanding, give more time, and give the benefit of the doubt to horses who seem to just be resisting, because I remember many times when I didn't know a horse was in pain.

I'm not here to tell you how to feel, but I am here to tell you that you can think of guilt as a positive sign of moving forward, of being able to empathize with other people and with horses, and that you can use it to find a happier outlook.

Speed and Fear

Many riders all around the world suffer from a common ailment: fear in the saddle. This fear is often exacerbated by the faster gaits, or only appears at the faster gaits. Many of my students explain to me apologetically that they struggle with fear but know they "need to get over it."

I think there are many layers to this issue, and just telling folks to "stop being afraid" by practicing more is about as useful as telling someone in the midst of a panic attack to calm down. Fear is a useful tool that tells us when something is not right. Fear, if looked at correctly, is not the problem but the symptom. Furthermore, many teachers of riding can't empathize with fear (which is lucky for them, since riding is their job, and fear would be a large hindrance). Teaching a fearful student is something many teachers feel frustrated by because their students can't just "get over it."

Let's examine some of the layers of fear in riding, as I've most commonly observed. There are countless, of course, but these are the observations based on my own experience.

• **Many riders don't get the benefit of learning to ride on educated, quiet, balanced horses.** I don't mean just the gentle older plunk at the school barn who shuffles along while you learn to post. I mean a horse whose trot and canter are supremely balanced, and the beginning rider can learn what that balance in the upper gaits feels like while they gain their own bearings.

This is an incredibly rare experience for most of us. The most educated horses are reserved for upper-level riding, and those at the beginning stages ride horses who just don't toss people that often. So riders become accustomed to horses that are heavy on the forehand and kind of dull, and they don't learn to ride with balance, feel, and good timing. They learn to just survive on horseback.

Worse yet, many riders with less experience are riding horses with little experience too. This is a very troubling situation I unfortunately encounter quite often: someone who maybe does not realize the precarious situation they are in, on an uneducated horse, stumbling around in the woods together. Of course, in this instance, fear is 100 percent rational. This rider isn't prepared to ride the erratic movements of the green horse, and the green horse is not prepared to be ridden by a newbie rider, and in many cases, is not prepared to be ridden by anyone.

- **Many off-balance horses feel safe at the walk, but become quick, worried, and unbalanced at the canter.** The horse knows that falling is a risk, and they protect themselves through bolting, bucking, or stopping quickly, for example. The rider fears these movements and tries to restrain the horse, exacerbating the problem. Many riders seem to intuitively know this, and therefore keep their work at the walk and trot, while feeling bad that their fear is the cause of limiting canter work.

- **Instructors who don't understand the root cause of this fear, or who can't empathize with it, push fearful riders to practice more cantering.** As well-meaning as this is, fearfully practicing cantering does not produce relaxed cantering. As we know from our work with horses, just repeatedly pummeling them with fearful stimuli makes them (a) more fearful, (b) not adaptable or trusting, and (c) shut down, because they are eventually forced to do what you want to get you to leave them alone. Students, too, need the empathetic training of building the necessary blocks of good riding basics and confidence, and cantering often takes care of itself.

• **Accidents, spills, and wrecks—along with the aforementioned list, falls are the nail in the coffin.** We're hardwired to remember negative experiences for survival. Horses are this way too. If you had 10,000 good rides and one spill, you forever remember what led up to that spill and become deeply suspicious of similar conditions from then on. Understanding that, we can gently and carefully learn to reprogram our minds, along with acquiring the necessary tools to deal with that scenario again. If you fell off because your horse bolted at the mounting block, maybe 10,000 repetitions where you and your horse just learn to breathe together at the mounting block is exactly what you both need.

So how do you conquer your fear? The cure for fear is a good seat, preparation, honest assessment, and a well-educated horse. Here are three key points to remember:

• **Learn the basic and foundational and super-duper-important elements of a good seat.** I can't stress this enough. Get a good, balanced seat and never stop working on it. It's not always easy to find access to a school master, but if you can, jump on the opportunity! Taking lunge line lessons on a finished horse can do wonders for your confidence. Don't make excuses for your riding skill, as if "I'm just a trail rider" or "I don't show" were a reason to not ride well. Equitation will benefit your confidence, your horse's confidence, and could save your life.

• **Get a good instructor, a therapist, a sports coach, a life coach, or all of the above.** Learn to teach your mind how to find a calm center, and learn to feel your horse. Learn to feel your horse's movement, read expression, and build tools for responding, riding, and guiding your horse with confidence.

• **Don't skip out on training and honest evaluation.** If you had an accident, get help for your horse too. They can become deeply traumatized by a spill, even if they weren't hurt. Find some help from someone who can bring your horse back to confidence and help you get back up there with confidence. Get your horse's canter super balanced. Take all the time in the world, but be willing to accept that your horse may not be suitable for you.

Is Your Horse Wrong for You?

Is your horse "wrong" for you, or do you just need to keep working at it? That's a great question, requiring lots of pondering, and I think nobody has the right to make that decision for you but you. But here are some ideas to help you determine your choices:

- What are your goals? Can your horse meet those requirements? If the goals are unreasonable, can they be changed to suit the horse?

- Do you feel scared more often than not? Is this something that gets better as you learn more, or is it something you can't shake? Is it destroying your love of riding? Do you hate going to the barn, and are you losing interest? Or do you find yourself wanting to make it work?

- Is your safety at risk? This is a huge one. Some horse-and-rider combos are just not ideal because the rider (and horse) are at risk. Even if your desire to learn is great, if the horse is quick to react and you are slow to react because of inexperience, this learning curve might be too great to be safe for you.

- Do you have good help? Not just a good teacher but a support system? It's not impossible to do it on your own, but it can make a significant difference and give you a far better chance if you have a person or group of people supporting, directing, and rooting for you.

- Do you love this horse, or do you love the idea of conquering a challenge? Sometimes it can be really hard to admit that the horse might be better off elsewhere. Sometimes we get stuck in the idea of not failing—and our concern with this causes us to fail the horse. Other times, the horse is safest and happiest with us, and with some elbow grease, time, and dedication, miracles can happen.

The choice is highly individual and should not be accompanied by judgement. Doing what's best for our horses and ourselves can look different in everyone's unique situation, and what's right for one person is not right for others. It can be a hard choice to make, but an important one.

So you've decided your horse isn't the one for you. What's next? I believe that every horse can be helped with the right person. But the amount they can come around, considering the resources, skill level, time, money, and desire, is really the limiting factor. I've worked with thousands of troubled horses, and these things are what make or break their ability to get along with people in a home.

If you've decided to let go of your riding partner, their future is somewhat daunting. Will they get along safely and happily with someone else? Is their well-being improved or worsened if you sell them? Can they be a pasture pet? If they can't, is it really ethical to bounce them from one precarious situation to another? So many questions and ethical dilemmas involved. I personally own four previously troubled horses who will never leave my home because, while they get along great here, I know it wouldn't take much for them to fall apart, even with a kind, well-meaning person. So they are either ridden by me, or they are pasture pets for the duration of their lives.

Not everyone has the financial means to keep a pasture pet, but we do make a commitment to them when we take them on to care for them. Again, there is no one answer, and the solution is highly personal.

The Truth

The truth will set you free, but first it will piss you off.
—Gloria Steinem

I have been working with troubled horses for long enough to see a common thread in their rehab process: feelings get hurt. Sometimes I think I need to get a degree in psychology to really be good at this. The solution for the horse is often quite simple: change our habits, change their environment, make consistent rules, and learn along with our horse.

The human factor is not so simple, however. First we have to accept the reality of the situation and our contribution to the problem. The human mind is expert at rationalizing, excusing, and then when it accepts, it beats itself with the truth. None of these are constructive habits, but meanwhile the horse waits in the background while we work on getting our sh*t together.

Guiding people through the process of seeing the truth as it is, without being mad about it, hating themselves for it, blaming others, lashing out, shutting down, becoming fearful, or losing interest entirely is really quite something. I've learned a lot about myself and my habits as well. Not taking this process personally is a goal I hope to achieve someday, but I get to understanding and empathizing with it more as I gain more experience.

My intention toward horses and people is always to help create a better life for them. But in that process, walking the fine line between being truthful and sympathetic toward someone's feelings is a tightrope act, and sometimes feelings do get hurt.

The Blame

Why is it so hard to accept personal responsibility in our learning journey? We are always blaming things outside ourselves for our problems: the weather, distractions, the time, other people, the horse, you name it. We all do it to a certain degree.

I remember a teacher I very much admire and respect telling me that I was drilling my horse. I responded that I was not drilling the horse, I was practicing for my own ability. He said that the two were the same to the horse, and my efforts to be a goal-achieving, driven rider were causing stress to my horse.

I don't know why that was so hard to swallow. It conflicted immediately with the image I had of myself. Then, when I accepted it, I felt shame. Then I felt like giving up. In reality, it's not that big of a deal—if I just had accepted the information and changed, without having to go through the twisted labyrinth that is the human ego, I could have moved along happily.

I'm really glad horses are here to help show us the way to be better people. I'm glad they put up with us while we flounder through life. I think taking criticism gets a little easier—to not ignore it or smash yourself over the head with it is tough, but essential.

Taking Responsibility

Troubled or lame horse? It's time we as a horse community take responsibility. There is an enormous amount of lame and troubled horses in the world as a by-product of poor horse keeping, unethical breeding, and poor handling. It might not be your fault the horse is suffering from these bad practices, but if they're in your care, it's your responsibility.

The likelihood that a magical person will appear to take this horse of yours and transform them into a happy horse living up to their full potential is rare. You might get lucky and find a rescue, or a kind soul who wants the project or is happy to have a pasture companion. But more than likely, while you wait for this mystery person to appear and solve your problems, the horse is suffering mentally and physically without getting the support they need.

We need to take responsibility for the lives that suffer from us. Can you afford the rehab, time, and training of a compromised horse? While no one covets euthanasia, rest is not the worst thing that can happen to a suffering horse.

If you invest in the training, you need to maintain the habits and work that your horse needs to be happy. You can't just throw money at a problem; you need to change your lifestyle to suit the horse, or let them find peace. Nobody is going to solve the problem of your troubled horse for you. Not even a great trainer can fix the horse if you stand in the way of progress. If they're in your care, they're counting on you.

We need to take responsibility for the lives we bring into our own—they can't live a happy life without us making some big changes.

Learning to Feel

Why can't you feel what your instructor said is going on? For starters, there's nothing wrong with you. I'm guessing most riders who say they felt what their instructor pointed out are not being honest. They're afraid to look like an insensitive, unintelligent, incompetent rider. But of course that isn't the case if you don't feel anything—learning to feel the entire body of a horse moving under you is really something difficult. There are a few things I think that affect this ability to feel in major ways.

Firstly, beginning instruction focuses mainly on teaching the rider to control the horse. We learn to pull to steer, kick to go, and become concerned far too soon with directing a moving, breathing, thinking animal we don't even understand. We're told to be the leader before we even know how they think, what it feels like to follow their gaits with our seats, and how to understand their needs. Thinking of controlling this soon doesn't develop our ability to feel.

Secondly, a huge portion of feeling what is currently going on is actually made possible through contrast. If you're accustomed to a flat-moving, imbalanced horse, that feels normal to you. A small change in balance isn't going to be so obvious. But if you ride a big mover, then a small mover, an uphill horse, a downhill horse, a tight horse, a loose horse, a happy horse, and a miserable horse, suddenly those differences are quite noticeable. What else can you do to feel the little details more easily?

• **Play around with closing your eyes.** If you feel safe, ride with your eyes closed. Obviously, do it in an enclosed space, have someone lead your horse, or do whatever you need to feel relaxed. You'll be surprised at what you pick up on when you deprive yourself of your vision. Suddenly the horse moving under you is more dynamic—the footfalls are easily heard, and the way their back moves is easily felt.

• **Ride different horses if you can.** A good seat is adaptable. We get caught up easily in our habits, and riding a variety of horses can help us learn to communicate in the moment instead of making assumptions with our seats.

• **Take video of yourself riding.** Most of us have smartphones. Put your phone on the fence and record your ride. It's quite eye-opening to see the difference between what we think is happening versus what is actually happening. Through seeing this, you can adjust your ability to feel over time. I video myself at least once a week. It isn't always fun or pleasant, but it's very helpful. Get a glass of wine handy and watch the video with an open mind.

Stress

Stress and discomfort tend to get a bad reputation in our comfort-and-happiness-obsessed society. But stress and discomfort are not inherently bad. You have to stress muscles to grow them. You have to stretch your comfort zone (i.e., get uncomfortable) to grow your skills and abilities. We can't run from stress and discomfort, especially since they are a reality for most of our lives. It's what we choose to do with these feelings that makes the difference.

Those of us who own horses know that they are easily stressed. A quick look through history, however, proves that horses are extremely adaptable. They have been used for war and travel, farming, hunting, and everything in between. All these required horses to step out of their comfort zone. In order for this to happen, people had to be willing to step out of theirs too.

If you let your own feelings about stress and discomfort limit you, they will also inevitably limit your horse. Obviously there are some ways more ethical than others to expose a horse to a variety of things. We can build on the old ways of having working horses while still treating them as sentient beings. We live in an unpredictable world. The best thing you can do for your horse is prepare it for stress, and teach it to be adaptable.

Post-delivery Discovery

I've been horseback since I was a little girl and have always ridden without apprehension. As a six-year-old, I jumped three-foot jumps on fire-breathing Thoroughbreds. I rode hot horses and rehabbed "problem" lesson horses as a teen. Fear hasn't really been part of the bag of emotions I carry on the saddle with me. Even while pregnant, though I rode more carefully, I rode without worry.

But after I gave birth, I found that climbing back in the saddle felt completely different. I expected it to be like dusting off the old bike and taking it for a spin; once you got going, it would all come back. Instead, my core was wobbly and unstable after being obliterated by nine months of carrying and then delivering an eight-and-a-half-pound baby. When my mare jigged a little and snorted at a car behind the trees, my instability made me nervous. I wasn't able to help her when she needed me, because I was busy worrying about myself.

Without core muscles to stabilize me, to absorb and compensate for unexpected movement, I felt nervous for the first time in my life. The urge to grab reins ran through my mind. Instead, I hopped off and did some lunge work to relax both her and myself. I realized I would need to take better stock of my current physical situation before riding more.

The thought suddenly occurred to me: physical as well as mental instability is really the mother of fear. Add to that a certain lack of knowledge—knowledge of the horse's movement and behavior—and you have the perfect storm. A horse, being a flighty prey animal, needs to move. If the rider can't stay with these potentially unpredictable movements, the horse's confidence drops. Or worse: if the rider grabs the reins, the horse now feels trapped and can easily panic.

Anyone who rides frequently knows that riding is far more than "active sitting." Confidence in the saddle comes from being able to follow the horse's movements at the walk, trot, and canter, and being stable enough to go with unexpected movement without stiffness or resistance. Good riding requires mental flexibility and the serious self-control to not grab, pull, or act impulsively in a way that would discomfort the horse. Good riding requires a solid understanding of equine behavior too—knowing why and when they feel the way they do, and helping to direct their behavior in productive and safe ways.

My conclusion after having a baby: riders who are unstable and green to horse psychology have every right to be afraid. In fact, without being in shape and knowing the ins and outs of horses' minds, riding is downright stupid. The remedy? Hop out of the saddle and spend some time on the mat. Work to develop strength, flexibility, and symmetry. Learn about directing your horses. Develop humane training tools focused on guiding, instead of fear-based control methods. Your safety and confidence depend on it. Without them, a good partnership with your horse will remain out of reach.

As for me? I'll be working on getting both me and my horses back in shape, and taking stock in where we are without making assumptions again.

Understanding, the Rx for Fear

A client recently asked me why I was not afraid when working with her horse. Rosinante lunged at me, kicked at me, and tried to bite me. She said she was afraid of him. Why wasn't I? He was now standing peacefully and with a soft eye while we groomed him. He was not the horse he once was.

I thought about it for a while before answering. Finally, I said I'm not afraid of him because I understand him. He's only behaving how he learned to behave, how he thinks he needs to behave to get by. Being afraid of him would do him a tremendous disservice and would keep me out of the moment, unable to think clearly and react. Rosinante's behavior wasn't personal. Though his front feet were aimed at me, he viewed his entire world as a threat. I imagine living life that way and can see how deeply unhappy he must have been. I don't waste my time with fear because I'm busy trying to change his life.

When you understand the horse's mind and have a good idea of what causes his behavior, fear tends to go away. Imagine being on an airplane for the first time and hearing the loud engine, seeing the wing flaps lift, and feeling sudden turbulence. If you don't understand how airplanes work, or the purpose of these sounds, it'd feel scary. Similarly, when people don't understand horses' expressions or what causes their behaviors, they may get afraid.

Fear is warranted when you understand what you see but lack the skill to do much about it. Fear is nature's way of expressing danger, and it's important to listen to that feeling. However, with knowledge and skill, you have the power to eliminate a feeling that can take control and overpower common sense.

"Don't be afraid" is among the worst pieces of advice I've ever heard. If you fear working with a specific horse, or maybe all horses, get some help. Find a good coach who can walk you through exercises that build your knowledge base and confidence. Start small, maybe work with a horse that does not bring up fear in you. Find tasks that help you learn to see expression in the horse and the behaviors associated with unsafe situations. Learn how to confirm that behavior or redirect it. If you see relaxation building on the horse, that's one you'd want to confirm. If you see fear, tension, or distraction learn to redirect to something better, ideally before those behaviors exhibit themselves.

When you have knowledge and skill under your belt, you have the freedom to be spontaneous, flexible, and, most importantly, mentally quiet. Without the voice of fear distracting you, saying "what if" in the background, you can accomplish so much.

As for the horse that bit, kicked, and lunged at me? Rosinante no longer does those things. Months of being redirected to more positive behaviors have shown him how to be happy, relaxed, and engaged in his work. Fear on my end would have kept me out of the moment and kept me from helping him.

Long-Suffering Basics

Why do the basics take so long? The basics actually don't take much time at all. Teaching a horse and rider the building blocks of balance and relaxation is not that difficult or complicated, as long as both are a blank slate. What takes so much time is undoing poor basics, undoing poor movement patterns, and letting go of the wrong muscle memories and building the right muscle groups.

I've been riding with my teacher for almost a decade now. The first few years I barely made any progress, not because the work wasn't good, but because I didn't understand what she was even talking about. It went right over my head, and every lesson I had we sort of repeated the work of the last. My poor teacher repeated herself over and over, but I rode with others whose work undid what she was trying to do, and I just wasn't ready to understand it yet.

Then, when it clicked for me, I was all in, but my muscle memories, habits, and understanding were counterproductive. It took a long time (and I'm still working on it) to let go of the habits I had that stood in the way of progress. Same for my horses—they had habits that weren't helpful either, especially the habit of coming behind the bit: some of it wasn't my fault, some of it was. This was a very lengthy, uncomfortable, and down-right yucky phase. Not a lot of winning here. This is where most people quit—they find a new instructor because they aren't getting anywhere, or they bounce around to different "methods."

Then the breakthrough: I finally understood where she was coming from, what the benefits were, and my horses were starting to buy into it too. We were finding harmony, with beautiful moments sprinkled in, and getting successes to keep us motivated. This phase required lots of vigilance from my teacher and myself to not revert to old habits when we were tired, distracted, or learning something new.

After these new, more productive habits were better cemented, upward progress was possible. It took so long. Not because the learning itself was fated to be arduous, but because I was in my own way for much of the time. So why does it take so long? It doesn't. But we make it so—and there's nothing wrong with that process, because as Ray Hunt said, "You're not working on your horse, you're working on yourself."

Living Intentionally

When I teach people, I often get a long story from the student as part of the introduction. The story is intended to fill me in on the relevant details that might apply to today's lesson, but a common thing that happens is the story becomes long-winded, rambling through details that aren't relevant, sometimes leaving out details that ARE important, and ends up becoming kind of a monologue. They are often difficult for me to follow, and if people aren't redirected toward answering some specific questions, they might never end their stories.

Often our work with horses reflects the bigger picture in how we deal with our life as a whole. If we are stuck living in the past, without any kind of goal or even idea of how we got where we are, what "where we are" even is, or an understanding of what our role in it is, we can easily end up sort of floundering around. How can we direct the horse if we don't know what we want? How can we direct the horse if we aren't aware of what we're doing and how it affects the horse or the situation we're in?

Most people I work with say they want the horse to be their friend and partner. But a common thread among all people is that they aren't aware of themselves or their horse until undesirable things happen. They contribute just enough attention to get through it, then go back to coasting. Awareness, like any other skill, takes practice to become good at. Like a muscle, the more you flex it, the stronger it becomes. Without awareness, without intention, everything is happening "to" us, and we are the constant victim in our life's story.

Awareness begins with talking less, listening more. It begins with dropping the story and observing what is actually happening, now. The backstory can provide an understanding of where you are today, but it isn't an excuse, a trap, or something to coast on. Horses are remarkably adaptable if we allow them to be free from the past. They live in the now.

Start by simply noticing your own breath, then your horse's breath. Start observing and comparing, and try to drop the preconceived ideas you might have for the reality in front of you. It can be very freeing.

What a Young Horse Needs

The situation is a common and unfortunate one: a novice rider with little experience with youngsters finds a young partner. Maybe she was looking to save money. Maybe she wanted the experience of bringing a horse along. Maybe she just didn't know exactly what she was getting into. Suddenly, she finds herself in over her head with a frustrated, anxious youngster showing problematic behaviors. Now she finds herself becoming more fearful, losing confidence, and losing enjoyment in riding.

Not every rider and horse are a good match, and while some young horses are more gentle-natured than others, they often still get into trouble with amateur riders. I rarely recommend young horses for most riders. It takes a certain kind of rider to get along with a young horse, and many riders find themselves struggling despite plenty of saddle time and experience.

Young horses are wiggly, easily distracted or frustrated, and don't inherently understand the common riding aids we use. That inside leg and outside rein you're used to applying with an older horse might not affect this horse in the way you'd hoped. Your quiet trail ride might turn into a necessary training session, and if you turn it into a pulling match, the horse can learn some very unfortunate behaviors.

What I often find with riders and young horses is unreasonable expectations about how a young horse should behave under saddle and how they should respond to the rider's aids. They often are trying to ride them like older horses. Soon, both horse and rider are frustrated, and things go downhill fast. So what does a young horse need you to provide?

- A good idea of what you want them to do, with flexibility and adaptability for when things don't go well (as they will).
- A sense of humor and a sense of adventure. It takes a special type of person to laugh off a young horse's silly antics without pulling on them, and to redirect them to productive work.
- An understanding of how a young horse's mind and body operate, and a realistic expectation of physical and mental maturation. A rider of a young horse needs to know how to gently push her comfort level without leaving behind reality.
- Forgiving and forward hands. A young horse needs to be able to move, and when she moves faster or unexpectedly, she needs to be redirected, not grabbed.
- Variety in experience. A young horse needs interesting, different, and stimulating exposures. Just drilling in the arena is a very quick way to shut down a young horse's mind and sour her experience early on.
- A flexible and realistic timeline for development. Young horses don't need to worry about going to shows. And they aren't going to be trail masters anytime soon. You wouldn't send a kindergartener to college and expect them to sit through lectures quietly. Yet every day, young horses are expected to behave like perfectly mannered

adults, without the necessary time and skills needed.

What can you do if you have a young horse and feel in over your head?

- Engage in more groundwork. Avoid repetitive exercises and find novel experiences. Take in-hand walks and teach new skills.
- Find a teacher or trainer to help provide confidence for your horse where you feel unable.
- Keep learning and pushing yourself to be the kind of rider your horse needs.
- Consider rehoming your horse to a better-suited home, if you are unable to do these things.

Starting a young horse is simple if you follow some basic guidelines and keep a flexible frame of mind. But repairing the damage to a young horse who has lost confidence or who has learned unfortunate behaviors is not so easy. When riding a young horse, consider not just how she rides today, but how you'd like her to feel for a lifetime.

Making Resistance Beautiful

Get ready to be surprised. That's how I should preface my riding instruction with new students. One of my students told me, "You bring the opposite of everything I've ever learned, and it's constantly weird and surprising." That makes me smile, and I take it as a compliment.

But one of my philosophies gets the most perplexed looks: Use the horse's resistance and make it beautiful. Stop trying to make them not resist. I experience this issue with students frequently when it comes to their horses wanting to drift to the gate or refusing to go into the scary parts of the arena. The riders' instinct is to wage war. They need to either push the horse into the scary areas, force them away from the gate, or "make the wrong thing hard" by working them harder in areas they try to go.

These tactics are excessively confrontational. They may work in the short term, but the side effects make it the wrong way to solve a problem. Say you get your horse off the gate with heavy leg and rein aids. It worked. But what did the horse learn? Heavy leg and rein aids are required, and they should resist you until they ultimately concede. At this moment, most riders stop riding. Their seats become stiff while their hands go to work. This causes the horse's back to stiffen, making staying at the gate, in fact, the easiest thing for the horse. You end up building a braced horse, a resentful horse, a distrusting horse.

Many horses, while being pulled away from a gate, learn to add power to their underneck and shoulders to be used against the inside rein. In the end, if the horse does go away from the gate, their mind and body are not working together. You may get a mechanical response, not a soft one. The "make the wrong thing hard" approach is a bit more baffling to me. My first questions to students are the following:

- Why would you want to make work a punishment?
- If rest is the reward and work is aversive, at what point does that backfire when you go back to (good) work?
- Why would what you ask a horse to do be unpleasant one minute, then when you've moved on from the gate, say, magically become pleasant again?
- Why is it kinder to operate under the threat of more work than to simply force the horse to do what you want in the first place?
- With either tactic, even if you get what you want, how much time did you spend with a tight, imbalanced, braced, confused, or unhappy horse?
- Why are those ways of riding worth doing if you have alternatives?

My goal with every horse is to make work pleasant, to build a balanced, happy horse, and to set horses up for success for whatever they may encounter. This requires a two-pronged approach that goes from the general to the more specific:

- **Look at the overall picture.** Why does your horse want to go to the gate, and why doesn't he want to go into the corners? Maybe the issue is your relationship, the way you ride, your idea of arena work, or your horse's understanding of the aids. The horse may benefit from an arena break altogether. There are so many possibilities here, but often the problem we get stuck on is not the problem at all but a symptom of a larger problem.

• **Prepare your horse to handle unfamiliar situations.** The horse may benefit from being hand-walked into the scary areas and learn to relax there. The horse might not understand how to get straight and is just looking for something to lean toward, and the gate is an easy draw. More groundwork and in-hand work might be needed. If you're prepared and have considered the Big Picture, then take the horse's resistance and make it productive and beautiful.

What are some practical applications of this approach? If my horse avoids a corner, for example, that is a perfect place to teach shoulder out or leg yield away from that corner. If the horse is green, I can use those areas to begin preparation work for lateral movements, of riding a large circle but on a counter bend. In this way, we are moving away from the scary areas but with purpose. Not only do I get to use their natural movement to teach something easily, they can become straighter and more supple because of it. Eventually, as we pass these areas in the arena, they become less and less concerned and more focused on the work. Soon enough, these areas are not a problem at all, and we can leg yield wherever we want.

How does this apply to sticking to the gate? This is an excellent opportunity to improve your horse's understanding of rhythm. I normally focus where I intend to move toward as I relax my reins, keep the rhythm in my body, and ask the horse to maintain the rhythm too. When ridden correctly, a horse in rhythm not only cannot stick at the gate, but in feeling more secure, he begins opening up his shoulders. Best of all, he is directed by not fighting with the rider. Everyone wins.

People think of these strategies as "letting the horse get away with things." I don't see horses ridden this way as getting away with things, but rather learning to trust their rider who consistently directs with fairness, prepares them well, provides a good feeling in all work, and makes the horse better physically and mentally with each ride.

Contact Is the Gift

In the culture of dressage, many riders think of contact as the first priority. When their ride begins, they pick up the reins and only loosen them at the end when riders dismount. "The horse has to learn to accept the contact" is the phrase I hear. Young horses started in dressage are often, unfortunately, lunged with side reins before being ridden to teach them to accept contact before learning how to carry themselves or even how to be steered. Riding on a loose rein, or even loosening the reins periodically, puts one at risk of being called "not a real" dressage rider.

Yet the dressage training pyramid begins with rhythm, relaxation, and then connection. The first priority is not contact, but rhythm and relaxation. When a horse has these two qualities, contact is something the horse offers you, not something the horse has to accept.

When ridden into relaxation with rhythm, the horse can willingly reach for the bridle and happily connect to the rider's hand. Considering contact as something the horse must accept is just another way of saying you expect submission. It says: "Here is uncomfortable, meaningless pressure that I expect you to deal with without argument." Why do riders say this? Riders with this mentality don't understand the purpose of dressage.

Dressage done well, with classical values, has the purpose of straightening, strengthening, and elasticizing the horse. Think of it like physical therapy for the horse's body. It isn't exclusive to expensive horses, big movers, calm horses, or riders who can afford $200 breeches and custom boots. Dressage is the art of making your horse the most comfortable they can be with the goal of longevity. Dressage should improve horses' soundness and overall quality of life. It should protect the mind of the horse. If your priority is submission and a certain head and neck shape, that original purpose of dressage is not possible.

When it comes to teaching students to ride horses into a balanced, willing contact, trail and Western riders are often easier pupils than riders with dressage backgrounds, who have heavy hands and a strict mindset around contact. With the latter, I often must substantiate my dressage experience as the contact method is unfamiliar. It's hard to teach a mind so closed, and it's hard for a horse to soften to a hand so hard and fixed.

I want hand and leg aids to be something the horse loves, something they seek. When rhythm and relaxation are put first, they can do this. My seat can feel good to them because their backs are not tense. They will enjoy following where my seat guides them. With my hands, I can offer contact as something to reach toward and take when they are ready, just as you can stretch out your hand for someone to take once they trust you.

Contact happens on the horse's time. Contact, done well, has a feel that is pleasant for both parties. It is dynamic and stride for stride, not something you hold in one place. Good contact is like dancing with the horse's mouth; there is give-and-take, breathing room, and the utmost respect for the mouth of the friend who allows you into their life. Contact is a gift your horses give you, not something you greedily take from them.

When Slow Is Worse

I've written a lot about going slowly and taking the horse's time. But did you know it's possible to go too slowly? Sometimes it can be just as damaging as going too fast. Going slowly isn't good on its own. You must go slowly with timing and knowledge.

Sometimes a client will bring me a horse to work on a problem that has an easy fix. The problem could have been eliminated immediately had the client understood what they were looking at and had the timing to fix it. Sometimes they want to be kind and soft, but, as a result, they become ineffective. The horse continues with the undesirable behavior, and the client ends up nurturing a wrong frame of mind. This frame of mind is carried into all the work they do together, and over time it cements. The problem that might have been a five-minute fix becomes a deeply ingrained habit.

For example, I once trailer-loaded a horse after a clinic after his poor owner had struggled for hours to get him on. As she led him up the ramp, he would tip his nose away from the trailer and his entire body would follow, taking him away from the trailer. In the interest of going slow and being patient, she would circle him around and try to load again. He kept repeating this behavior. It became worse and worse. Soon, he wouldn't go anywhere near the trailer. When any pressure was put on him to walk forward, he became very reactive. In his mind, this is exactly what he was supposed to do.

If his crookedness had been corrected immediately, he might have walked right on. When I came over to help load him, I focused on keeping him straight. As soon as I got him thinking about staying straight, he loaded up and stayed there. I gave him all the time in the world to think and to make choices, but I was quick to block options that would lead to him being more confused about getting in the trailer.

Another example involves green horses: while it's important to go slowly with young horses, you don't want to move at a pace that can cause boredom and lack of interest. If you repeat the same work every day, they learn to tune out or find coping behaviors, such as chewing on rope or reins; wandering on the lead line; or exhibiting inattentiveness, dullness, or overreaction to outside stimuli. Horses that aren't focused often spook more. Introducing new things frequently to a young horse can be very beneficial, provided the horse is not too anxious about it.

Going slowly is not beneficial if you're missing important details and not correcting elements that lead to bigger problems, or if the horse is bored or inattentive, or if your timing is off. Going slowly is especially detrimental if the horse is getting worse, not better.

Give your horse time to think and adjust. But don't wait forever if their attention has left, or if they're working on the wrong things. Guide gently, be flexible, and most importantly, be effective.

The "L" Word

Quite often I hear horses who are not freely forward described as "lazy." There are a few problems with this.

First, "lazy" is an anthropomorphic description. Horses don't care about our ideas of work ethic, or even know what those are. Their priorities are to eat, be secure in a herd, and look out for danger. Their priorities are not inside leg to outside rein, they don't care about doing straight flying changes, and they certainly don't care that you have a show coming up. The only way they can become invested in your work is if it makes them feel good—as in, brings them mental and physical well-being. Otherwise, you can threaten with your leg all you want and inspire a fear response, but they aren't lazy—they just don't share your priorities.

Second, most sluggish horses are extremely tight. Moving forward with a rider on their back is actually double or triple the amount of work that it should or could be. They are moving with a tight back, tight shoulders, and weak abs and haunches. Likely the rider is tight too, and quite likely the rider is not balanced as well as they could be and is using reprimanding or nagging aids. This horse is working FAR harder than they need to be.

If a horse's shoulders are supple, the back is free to lift, the core is engaged and working without interference, hind legs are swinging at optimum range of motion, movement is easy and enjoyable. So your "lazy" horse is far outworking a horse with looseness and alignment, because they have to work much harder just to go forward.

Imagine being pulled off your couch, given a 70 lb. pack to carry that slips around and isn't stable, and being asked to move forward through a series of obstacles without being fit or knowing how to position yourself. You aren't going to be moving very fast either, and someone nagging you to speed up incessantly will probably make you quite resentful. Something to think about next time you whip out the "L" word, which in my barn is a very dirty word, along with "stubborn."

What a Horse Endures

Since I had my daughter, I've had back pain. Not terrible enough to stop me from working, but enough to make me cranky at the end of the day. I've worked a full day's load with it just about every day since she was born, and it hasn't gotten better. (I'm going somewhere with this, you aren't reading my angsty diary, and this isn't a complaint session, I promise.) I've iced it. I've used heating pads, Bengay, massage, and stretching. I get temporary relief, but every day it comes back. I work out, I'm active, and I like to think I take decent care of myself (aside from being a terrible, mean, and ruthless overlord of me).

Over the last week, I've decided to get dedicated to doing yoga again. If you're familiar with the practice of yoga, you know its focus is on body alignment, strength, and lengthening of the body, and on creating an awareness of breath and body together. My back pain isn't gone entirely, but I sure do feel better. I feel more aware of my posture, more inclined to move in good posture throughout the day, and some tight, angry muscles are starting to release.

Why does my back hurt? Probably nine months of carrying weight around with poor posture around the weakest part of my back, plus a quick return to work with that same weak and poor posture, bad shoes, not enough stretching, and not enough attention to the deep postural muscles that allow my core to take over doing the job that my low back has been bearing the brunt of.

Where am I going with this? Almost every horse I meet endures some degree of pain. People often say with surprise, when a horse's pain is pointed out, "But he gets massage/chiropractic/bodywork!" I'm sure those things bring relief, and help, but if you aren't addressing the cause of the pain, it's only temporary relief. What does a horse endure? Weak and poor posture, poorly fitting saddles, imbalanced riders, imbalanced teeth, imbalanced or irregular hoof care, lack of movement, imbalanced diet—you name it.

Imagine being incredibly weak, being nine months pregnant, wearing boots that don't fit well, and having another kid on your back pulling your head around. I bet that's what horses feel like often, and I can't imagine most of us being very happy about that situation. If your horse has a poor topline with a weak core, a hanging belly, a tight neck and shoulders, a poorly fitting saddle, and a crooked rider (let's face it, we're all crooked), the massage is a drop in the bucket of pain management.

Address the root of the problem, develop a happy horse over time. I think of dressage as "horse yoga." Like yoga, you have strength with grace—stability and flexibility working together for the health and alignment of the horse. So don't skimp on the bodywork, by any means. But don't think it erases the snowball of pain your horse endures daily.

Dressage Is for All Horses

I remember hauling my rented two-horse trailer with my old green beater truck to dressage clinics. It was winter and my hairy horse in her full January coat stuck out among the clipped, immaculate warmbloods like a sore thumb.

The lessons usually involved (expensive) criticism of my horse. "She's just not built for dressage" was probably the least hurtful thing I heard. The obsession with image and whispers among auditors made me feel like I wasn't good enough and didn't fit in with the dressage crowd. I didn't have enough money, didn't have a good enough horse, and didn't belong. I felt like dressage was not for me.

I found a new teacher and a new crowd. My teacher, Theresa, never bats an eye at anything I bring her. I've ridden mustangs, warmbloods, Arabians, quarter horses, Morgans, and Iberians with her. The longtime student of Egon von Neindorff shows up to teach me in whatever setting I have, in comfortable clothes, and gives her all to improve the well-being of every horse she meets.

Dressage is for all horses, and true stewards of the horse can see each horse's individual needs and balance. We aren't going to the Olympics, but week by week we are happier together, finding suppleness and balance, and enjoying our work more. Dressage is for everyone—whether you can afford the imported warmblood or have a $500 horse from the auction. If you don't feel like you're good enough for the sport, you're in the wrong crowd.

My quarter horse, Dee, is a great example of this. She's sounder today at 15 than she was when I got her at 8, because of dressage. She was lame enough at 8 that I considered euthanizing, and now we are working on developing piaffe steps on a happy, confident horse. If I'd have given up because of the discomfort I felt in the stuffed-up environment I was in, she wouldn't be here today.

True Impulsion

Is your horse actually lazy, or is he stiff and heavy on the forehand, having learned to shut out your aids? Is your horse actually forward and hot, or is she nervous, off-balance, overstimulated, and frustrated?

True impulsion, to me, means directable energy. If you have energy you can't control, you don't have impulsion, you have worry. Being "in front of the leg," to me, means that the horse's front legs are literally in front of yours. If their forehand is tight, their front legs will take stiff, quick, choppy steps beneath them, as opposed to out in front of them. If your horse isn't forward, chasing him with driving aids will only create more tense, choppy steps but will not fix the problem. There is a big difference between being faster and generating more impulsion.

Often we look at the forward and slow types of horses as different, but they both are showing symptoms of the same problem: stiffness and lack of balance. Both horses can be helped with suppling the shoulders, lengthening and straightening the neck, and developing a swing through the back.

That's Just How We Do Things

One of the interesting parts of teaching the public and working with equine behavior "dilemmas," I'll call them, is running up against tradition. When it comes to behavior issues, often the problem can be quickly and simply solved with lifestyle changes for the horse instead of training. "That's just how we/they do things" is one of the most maddening and frequent responses I get. People at that point are looking for magic fixes—if you can't change the lifestyle, how do I make the problems go away without giving the horse the necessary elements that make up physical and mental well-being?

One such situation is stalling. Though it is well researched and documented that horses are better off turned out with a herd eating forage for large parts of the day, many horses live in stalls still. Excess energy, frustration, anxiety, and stereotypies such as cribbing and weaving are often the direct result of time spent in stalls. As it comes to their physical health, breathing issues such as heaves, stiffness, lack of blood flow and oxygenation to muscle tissue, higher risk of injury, colic, and ulcers are directly linked to time spent in stalls.

In some places around the country and the world, turnout is not available. I understand the frustration of not having access to land and the ability to do self-care. In these situations, you have to do the best you can. More hay and more time hand walking or riding is ideal. Gut support and ulcer prevention or treatment is a great idea as well.

If you have the chance to turn out and are worried about their safety, comfort, or whether they will stay clean: you know the risks, and you know the benefits. Horses who spend more time in stalls tend to have poor balance, decreased proprioception, decreased social skills, and less ability to manage changes in terrain. This puts them at greater risk for injury. If they aren't used to turnout, you can start slow. Maybe behind with a small paddock and hand walks around the property to get the feel of the terrain. It may sound silly, but I've had horses new to turnout stumble down a small hill, or over a log, and become very fearful. Find them a calm friend and work up to full turnout and socialization.

Numerous studies, equine behaviorists, and equine advocates all agree: turnout and forage is the best way to create a happy, healthy horse. Yes, even an old horse. Even a show horse. Even an arthritic horse. So turn them out!

It Takes Two to Fight

Have you worked with horses who have been taught to fight? You didn't start them that way, but here they are. Everything is a fight. If you don't start it, they do. They don't want to be that way, but it's what they know. They have been shown the only way to comply is through intimidation and force. Now here you are not using those ways, and you have a strong horse bowling all over you, or trying to get away. This horse is not happy to do this—this horse is scared, worried, unconfident. They don't know how to get along with you.

I get horses like these all the time. The temptation to fix the problem with force is there, because it works, and it seems the horse is looking for it. But in the long run, it will never create softness, confidence, or partnership.

With these horses, the art of being neutral is essential. I teach them that there is no fight. You can't show them softness by speaking the language they came speaking—I change the game entirely. I am neutral: I can't be pushed or pulled, but that fight will dissipate when the horse realizes I'm not involved in it. When they are ready, we can have a whole new type of conversation.

Once they realize they don't have to fight with you to protect themselves, and they don't have to be bullied into doing what you ask, they will be much happier, more willing, and more interested in being around you.

Dee, the Fiery

When I met Dee, she had a pinched mouth, tight back, and hard eyes. The day I went to look at her, she took over a half hour to catch. I was looking to buy my first horse and was overwhelmed with excitement at the prospect. I'd always loved horses, but could never have one growing up. As an adult, I was never financially stable enough to have one, but now, the moment was right. I found a chestnut barrel horse across the country that caught my eye and booked my flight to go see her.

It was February in Idaho, and I picked my way over the frozen ground carefully, blowing on my frigid fingers to keep them warm. She turned her head away from me while I haltered, and I brought the sweaty horse into the barn to dry her off and get to know her better. I fell in love with her then, and I had no reason to. She was basically a runaway, angry and hot-tempered. She tossed her head against the tie-down she wore, she pulled on the bit, and she didn't want anything to do with me. I had her shipped out to Michigan and signed the bill of sale, completely smitten with my shiny red mare.

I wanted a relationship with her more than anything else. She had this strong spirit, this indomitable will. She pulled back, ran away, wouldn't load in trailers, and attacked the other horses in her pasture. She was fiery, and I found myself very quickly in over my head. I couldn't tie her to anything because she would pull it out of the ground. I couldn't get on her without her bolting. I was constantly getting complaints about her hurting her pasture mates from the boarding barn I kept her at. I couldn't trailer her out because she would not tie in the trailer, but if loose, panicked and ran around so much that she would inevitably come out bleeding from somewhere. I thought I knew how to handle horses, but I didn't know how to handle Dee.

I began taking her to clinics. I learned how to lunge her in circles, how to do one-rein stops, and how to back her up when she got ahead of me. All of these things were supposed to be a cure, to get the horse's mind right. Everyone else in the clinics seemed to have a handle on their horses, but Dee seemed to be getting worse. When she felt the rein coming for a one-rein stop, she grabbed the bit and locked her neck up, running even faster. When she got ahead of me and I wanted to back her up, she would lock her neck and pile drive forward. When she dragged on the lead rope and I wanted to lead her up with my flag, she set her feet like cement blocks into the ground. I felt hopeless and frustrated.

I would hand her over to the clinician for help, only to watch her get brutalized. Clinicians backed her up across the arena, jerking her lead rope repeatedly. They hobbled her, they laid her down, they spun her in circles, they tied her head. When she was returned to me, both of us felt worse, and her behavior would worsen.

Soon after, Dee became dead lame. She barely moved in her pasture. I began recruiting the help of bodyworkers and vets alike to find a solution. Her feet began to flare and chip up. She was miserable, but she was difficult for these poor professionals to work on. She wouldn't stand for acupuncture. She didn't tolerate blood draws or vaccines, and she scared the death out of most vets. Eventually, I was able to get her hocks x-rayed and found they were fusing. I felt completely dismayed—not only was my beautiful horse unhappy in her life, her body was failing too. I began feeding her joint supplements, gave her Previcox, did ten rain dances and said twenty Hail Marys, but it wasn't until her hocks finished fusing that she felt a little bit better.

Over time, she did settle a little, but she was always tough. She was hard to catch for years, ranging from ten minutes to an hour on average. I had clinicians and trainers chase her, round pen her, even had five people in a field flag her until she went to me. It worked only when these situations were set up perfectly, and only because it was her last resort. She no longer bolted under saddle, but she jigged, tossed her head, chewed the bit, did not accept the contact, and couldn't regulate her tempo. She was always fast, never settled still, and hated the reins.

It seemed she was improving a little, but we were never getting to the root of the problem. Her lameness was still intermittent, and her back was still like a rock. I began to think that was just how she was. It had been six years, and she was better, but still I could tell she was not happy.

The first time I rode her in a clinic with Theresa Doherty, I was deeply entrenched in the work involving tight circles, one-rein stops, and other forms of, in retrospect, very dominating work. Theresa was explaining how wildly unbalanced she was, and that the circles were putting her off balance and causing her anxiety. Her work was so far over my head that it just didn't click for me. She explained to me that the work I was doing relied on putting her off balance to create better behavior, and asked me at what point would I require her to be balanced later, after she was well-behaved? She explained that my horse could not relax until my work didn't threaten her safety. I didn't understand it then, but the seed was planted.

I began riding with Theresa as often as she would come up our way in Michigan, but in between felt lost. I knew what not to do, but I didn't know what to do. I made many mistakes, but I was so excited to feel an inkling of hope. Theresa would ask me to loosen the reins and not take Dee's neck out of alignment. She would ask me to breathe, to find a rhythm, and to trust my bolting horse so that she could trust me. I had so much to work on to help this horse, but over time, her neck would go down, and her ears would move softly. She began to breathe, and she could stand still calmly.

Dee's manic canters and trots slowly over time blossomed into a swinging, rhythmic gait. Her bulging bottom neck muscles relaxed and softened, while new topline muscles began to pop. Her eye was softer, her short, stiff neck grew longer and more graceful, she looked healthier. She almost looked like a whole new horse. One day, I went out to catch my mare for her lesson, and I noticed she did not run from me. For the first time in her entire life, she stood for me calmly to be haltered. I was so stunned I cried. Soon after that, she would approach me to be caught, with a soft eye. I knew we had stumbled onto something beautiful together.

To ride Dee now with her swinging back, soft tail, rhythmic breathing, steady footfalls, and buttery softness and receptivity to the bit is beyond a dream come true. It is all I ever wanted in life, and more. Not only is her face happier, but her body has completely changed. Her previously short, bulky neck is now long and graceful. Her legs are straighter and she stands square. Her once rock-hard back that felt like a slingshot is now like sitting into my favorite recliner. She is willing and calm, and often teaches my students to ride with a generosity and grace that just fills my heart with love.

I owe this horse everything I know, and beyond that, I owe her a lifetime of apologies for the suffering I put her through. She is brave, intelligent, strong, and cannot be forced, intimidated, or bullied. She is everything I hope to be. I often think, how lucky we are to have horses, and how wildly undeserving we are. I am grateful every day for Dee, and will keep trying to pay forward what she taught me.

Lindo, the Beauty

Before I owned him, Lindo had been stalled daily, with short amounts of time turned out in a private paddock. He wasn't well socialized, was anxious, went behind the bridle badly, and reared under saddle. When I got off, he would run backward, and when working in hand, he would completely stiffen up to the point of being unable to move, breathing rapid, shallow breaths from the moment I haltered him. He was extremely unconfident in all areas of life, and like Dee, he struggled with soundness.

His show scores from his competition days were in the low to mid 80s, which, in the sport of dressage, is quite high. The judge's comments often read things like "beautiful horse, lovely mover, needs relaxation," or "beautiful canter, work on fixing tension." He scored high in competition until he put the literal brakes on his career, stopping and rearing down centerline. His brain was fried, his body was nearly ruined, and his unhappiness was palpable.

I did nearly everything in my power and knowledge bank to help him. I turned him out with other horses, but he attacked them and then stood shaking at the gate. He wouldn't eat my hay, being accustomed to large portions of grain and dense alfalfa hay. He pawed at my gate, probably certain he would starve to death. Under saddle, he would barely move, and could not respond to any light aid—it was as if he could not understand unless the aid was severe, and then when given a severe aid, he would be afraid. He stumbled and fell to his knees on a loose rein. He couldn't navigate even a slight incline, pole on the ground, or trail. He hated being in a stall, but was terrified of other horses and the outdoors. He wasn't happy anywhere.

I tried to keep him barefoot in boots with pads, in hopes his severely damaged feet would heal. He was so uncomfortable in them that he wouldn't move. In shoes, he moved a little better, but it didn't solve the problem. His feet were weak, prone to fungus, and misshapen. His back was tense and he had inflammation in his sacroiliac (SI) joint. I treated him with frequent bodywork, anti-inflammatories, Adequan injections, magnetic blankets, and he would still stand like a stone. It was as if these methods to relax him could barely make it past the skin. One bodyworker commented that he seemed to be "rejecting" the work.

His movement was choppy, uneven, and very stiff. Often he limped badly under saddle, but would not limp in the pasture. His movement under saddle was so poor, I hypothesized, because he was habituated to tension, which made him "rein lame." In other words, his tension created poor movement patterns, but was not necessarily caused by a real physical problem. I knew he needed to relax in order to move better, but I couldn't seem to get him to relax at all.

My teacher insisted he needed to learn rhythm, but he wouldn't move. She said when he learns rhythm, he can unlock his back, and then he can breathe. I would make a little progress, and then he would lock up again, and we would be back to his limping. I gave him time off, tried different therapies, but my teacher insisted the problem would only resolve when he could move in rhythm.

She probably repeated the same thing to me in every lesson over the years I struggled with him—"Don't worry about making him faster, worry about making him rhythmic." I would think, how can I make him rhythmic if he won't *go*? How can I direct movement into balance when every step feels like rolling a boulder up a hill? My teacher would say, "Don't use your legs on his already tight rib cage! Use your seat!" I knew that overusing my legs wouldn't work, and he would stiffen against them and go even less, but he didn't respond at all to my seat with such a tight back. I felt frustrated, and the horse underneath me moved like a zombie with limbs that didn't bend.

One day, it finally clicked. It isn't at all about moving him forward faster—it's about getting the movement he offers balanced. We were moving at a snail's pace, and I finally just accepted it. Let's move slow, I said to him, but let's do it like a slow ballet. One, two, three, four, one, two, three, four. I suddenly found him rushing off, and then stopping abruptly. I kept counting in my head: one, two, three, four. In some time, he gave the smallest little shake of his head, the first indication of a release. I kept at it. One, two, three, four, one, two, three, four—this time counting out loud so I would not lose it. His neck went down, and there was a change in his back. In a few more minutes he let out a sneeze, and his tail relaxed. I could see his eye looking sleepy almost, and he pushed his nose in the dirt as he walked, like a bloodhound on the trail of something. He kept blinking, shaking his head, walking slow but steady. I could feel his hind legs under me, and suddenly there was a place for my seat to go, to melt into. I let the ride end there, feeling ecstatic.

It was hard not to get excited and push this horse, now that I could feel the potential for movement that he had. This was a brilliantly moving, well-bred horse. When he was locked up he felt absolutely awful, but once he was loose it was apparent that this was quite the horse. Each day I reminded myself that rhythm was my only goal. It took some time to get him back into this way of going for a few weeks, but then suddenly he was loose right off the bat, moving fluidly in long, graceful, ground-covering steps. It was only a few weeks after that where he was trotting in a beautiful, swinging stretch, blowing and blinking with the most gorgeous gait I could imagine.

Lindo's body changed dramatically over the next months. His skinny, upside-down neck grew into the beautifully developed neck of the stallions I'd ridden in Spain. I sometimes couldn't take my eyes off his neck, or the way he appeared to move between the trees of my pasture like a jungle cat, swinging through his whole body. He developed a much more peaceful appearance, and his feet developed a healthier shape.

It's still hard not to get excited about this gorgeous creature, and I'd be lying if I said there wasn't a greedy little gremlin in my ear, trying to convince me to take him to a show. Who wouldn't want to show a horse like this off? But I remind myself to take it one day at a time, to be grateful that Lindo is sound and happy, and to remember the purpose of this work is to improve the quality of his life. If we can trot down the centerline without compromising his mind or body, then we will do it. But for now, we will continue to walk and trot in flowing, rhythmic steps.

Marlin, the Strong

Marlin came to me originally as a training horse to be started under saddle. He was hard to catch, bolted on the lead line, and had a pretty impressive resume of dangerous and evasive behaviors. He was a ten-year-old mustang, and at the time, I didn't have much experience with mustangs, let alone mustangs that had been feral for a decade.

He came loose in a stock trailer, whirling around inside like a cartoon Tasmanian devil. I admired his balance and athleticism from afar—his ability to buck and spin within the confines of the trailer without losing his footing was impressive. I came to learn that he knew where his feet were at all times to a degree I hadn't seen before.

Catching him could take thirty minutes, an hour, or two hours. If he couldn't evade you, he would try to run over you. One time, he actually ran through the wooden boards of the round pen to get away; when I was finally able to catch him, he had quite the laceration on his front fetlock. I will never forget leaning down to clean and wrap his fetlock, like I was doctoring a wild cougar. I kept my eye on him, tentatively wrapping and waiting to have to jump back from a kick, strike, or bite. But he just stood there, eyeing me with a stoic calm. I had the feeling he knew when I was helping, such as doctoring a wound, and when I was a threat, such as trying to train him.

In almost every session for a few months, he bolted at some point. I would feel the rope come tight and know he was leaving, and I learned to just surrender to it. He would run off, and I would saunter after him to go get him again. It almost became a low-drama event, as if the two of us knew it was going to happen and we both had become calmer about it. I knew that tying him hard and fast wouldn't help much, after I watched him nearly hang himself on a patience pole some time earlier. I had seen all four of his feet come off the ground, neck extended straight up, and at no time did the fight leave his body. I knew he would fight to the death if necessary, and knew that working with him in that way would not be the way I wanted to go.

He bucked harder than I'd ever seen a horse buck, sometimes so hard he would fall down, flail, and get back up to do it again. He bronced around the arena at the presentation of a flag, rope, dewormer, or anything that aroused his suspicion. I tried my best to stay calm and remain neutral, though I rarely knew what to do.

Over time, he started to trust me a little bit more. He was getting easier to catch, less dodgy, and letting me trim his feet. He would sometimes place his nose on my shoulder and breathe on me if I sat down in the round pen. I felt it was time to get him ready to ride, so I began working on getting up and down with my foot in the stirrup. He accepted this with slight fidgetiness, but nothing out of the ordinary. Once I felt confident, I was getting ready to swing my leg over to sit in the saddle, with the intent of getting right back down. I put my toe in the stirrup, and without batting an eye, he turned and knocked me over with both hind feet.

I lay on the ground, expecting to find myself mangled, and wondered where my cell phone was. I wondered how long it would take for anyone to find me half dead in the round pen with a murderous mustang. But once my breath returned, I found myself uninjured completely. He had used just enough force with perfect aim to knock me off my intended course of action, but not enough to even leave more than two faint hoof-shaped bruises on my chest. He always knew exactly where his feet were.

I eventually did ride him, after I brought Dee into the round pen. I let her loose while I worked on getting on and off, and a few times when he shaped himself up to bolt or kick at me, she lodged her body directly in front of him. With his nose right over her back, he began to settle, and I made my way onto his back, rubbing his neck while he let down his guard.

I rode Marlin a total of twelve times. Every ride was a success, with no drama, but it was the kind of success I imagine a combat pilot feels after a safe landing: this time I made it, but maybe not so lucky next time. Marlin seemed to understand and accept what we were doing, and while I felt he trusted me, he always kept his guns loaded with his finger on the trigger. He had been an outlaw for all his life, and wasn't about to give up his autonomy or ability to defend himself if needed.

Marlin was eventually given to me, and though I didn't need another horse, I loved him at that point too much to let him out of my life. He lived with Travis and me and our other horses peacefully. One day, I was traveling home from Texas after a clinic and my husband called. Marlin had cut his side somehow, maybe on the fence, and it needed a vet. "Ok," I said, "have the vet out." I didn't think much of it and knew my husband could handle it.

A few hours later, Travis sent me a photo of the gnarliest wound I'd ever seen. After cleaning, it revealed an injury far more serious than Travis or the vet had realized. It required three layers of stitches and went from his shoulder all the way to his flank. He had to be loaded and hauled to the vet school, sedated, clipped, and stitched, and again, he was perfectly calm and easy for the vets to handle. He seemed to have a great sense of people's intentions, and had no tolerance for anything that didn't benefit him.

The vets gave his full recovery a slim chance, and worried that the stitches would not hold. In the heat of summer, infection was a big risk as well. Keeping him on stall rest was not an option, as he would have done far more damage to himself in a stall than grazing quietly in the field. We flushed the wound out twice daily, gave him antibiotic injections, and watched in amazement as he healed over time. He developed a large scar with lots of damage to the muscle tissue in the area, so we decided to retire him from riding.

I was partly sad to retire him, but honestly was just happy to have gotten him to the point where he was safe to lead, trim, and trailer. He became easier to catch all the time, and calmer. By the end of his life, he was the nicest horse on a lead line we had on the property. He was soft and responsive, and I often used him in lessons or classes to teach people how to draw the horse in and engage their interest in catching. Sometimes I used him to teach people how to lead or for other simple groundwork exercises.

There was so much I loved about Marlin. He had a beautiful, wavy mane, and a delicate yet manly head. He was a beautiful horse, strong for his size, with movement far nicer than his long back and upright pasterns seemed to indicate. He had a floating trot and a fluid, rocking-horse canter. But what I loved the most about him was that he never gave up his self-protection, and never did anything without being fully convinced it was in his best interest. There was no making Marlin do anything until he was 100 percent sure of it. I think what I took away from my time with him the most was that it was never fair to ask anything of a horse if you couldn't explain to them why they needed to do it, and that "just because" is never a good enough answer.

In Closing

Sharing this book with you is like sharing my diary, so I hope you will treasure it and treat it with the respect due someone coming out with a big secret. And not just my secret, but a big, ugly, collective secret of societal treatment.

The equine industry has fed on the hopes and dreams of many a starry-eyed, eager young person. It has produced both disillusioned and burnt-out people whose sensitivity and work ethic has proven to be their demise, and created calloused, hard, arrogant people, likely made so out of necessity for survival. This experience is not unique to me; it has happened to countless people.

We have all been there: the situation doesn't feel right. The work with the horse seems a little rough, or too much. The way they treated that person, or many people, makes your stomach sink. Everyone around you seems to be enjoying it or agreeing with it, but you just don't feel right about it. It's in our nature to not go against the crowd—most of us feel deep fear of rejection or being ostracized from our group. And if everyone around you doesn't mind it, who are you to say it's wrong? You doubt yourself, wonder if you are actually seeing what you're seeing, and think surely the professional, or whoever is doing it, knows more than you.

I believe real change takes two people: one to notice, and another to agree. One against a crowd is too much. But with one more person speaking up, or even agreeing with you, you can feel much more courageous. Two can make the change. One extra person can turn the tide. One more person can be the difference between disaster, ongoing abuse, and harm to horse and human. One person can help another person trust their knowledge, value their inner feelings, and feel safe again. One person can restore someone's confidence and prevent years of second-guessing and more abuse due to self-doubt.

There are many times I wish I'd had that person around, and many more times I wish I'd been that person. Now that I have a daughter, I think of past scenarios that I, or others, were involved in, and I ask myself, would I let that happen to her? Absolutely not. I would do anything in my power to protect her. But at the risk of sounding corny, we are all connected to each other—if we let it happen to someone else, what's to stop it from happening to us? Will you be that one extra person? I hope to be that person from now on.

Acknowledgments

To my husband, Travis, for celebrating the beautiful days with me, and for picking me up at the end of each tiring day. To my daughter, Josie, for making me laugh, smile, grow, and for teaching me to see life through a child's eyes. To Maddy Butcher, for planting the seed in my head about writing another book and making it a reality. To the readers of my articles, for emboldening me to keep writing about my thoughts. To my students, for their hard work and open-mindedness, and for sharing the beauty of riding with me. To my teachers and role models, Brent Graef and Theresa Doherty, for the light they shine in the horse world, and for helping to show the way. Special thanks to Jasmine Cope and Melinda Yelvington for their beautiful photos.

About the Author

Amy Skinner lives in North Carolina with her long-suffering husband, daredevil toddler, four good horses, and two nutty dogs. At her ranch, she starts young horses and rehabilitates emotionally and physically damaged horses. She is a clinician who travels the country teaching horsemanship and balanced riding. Amy is a lifelong student of the horse committed to becoming a better rider and a better human, every day. She is also a student of Brent Graef and Theresa Doherty, two humble and gifted human beings whose grace and ability to read horses inspire her.

Resources

Ballou, Jec Aristotle. Accessed September 30, 2021. https://www.jec-ballou.com/.

Dass, Ram. Last modified August 31, 2021. https://www.ramdass.org/.

Fundación Real Escuela Andaluza del Arte Ecuestre. Last modified September 29, 2021. https://www.realescuela.org/.

Graef, Brent. Last modified August 14, 2020. https://www.brentgraef.com/.

Hunt, Ray. *Think Harmony with Horses: An In-Depth Study of Horse/Man Relationship*. Edited by Milly Hunt. Bruneau, ID: Give It a Go Books, 1978.

Lenz, Tom. "Stall Confinement." *American Association of Equine Practitioners*. https://aaep.org/horsehealth/stall-confinement.

Loving, Nancy S. "Consequences of Stall Confinement." *The Horse: Your Guide to Equine Health Care*, April 1, 2010. https://thehorse.com/121297/consequences-of-stall-confinement/.

Rashid, Mark. Accessed September 30, 2021. https://markrashid.com/.

"Respect and Dominance in Training, Debunked." Tumblr, accessed September 30, 2021. https://animalwelfarists.tumblr.com/post/101634709325/respect-and-dominance-in-training-debunked/amp.

Tolle, Eckhart. Last modified September 16, 2021. https://www.eckharttolle.com/.

Von Neindorff, Egon. Last modified September 15, 2021. https://vonneindorff-stiftung.de/.

Watts, Alan. Last modified July 23, 2021. https://alanwatts.org/.

Made in United States
Troutdale, OR
04/06/2024

18986145R10072